NOTES FROM THE CLOSET

Stories of Women's Relationships from the 1930s through the 1990s

BARBARA ROSEMAN

American Literary Press, Inc.
Five Star Special Edition
Baltimore, Maryland

FOR A SPECIAL FRIEND

"But if you tame me," said the fox, "then we shall need each other. To me, you will be unique in all the world. To you, I shall be unique in all the world ..."

"I am beginning to understand," said the little prince. "There is a flower ... I think she has tamed me ..."

Antoine De Saint-Exupery

Table of Contents

Preface v

The 1930s
Teenage Crush 1

The 1940s
G. I. Gals 13

The 1950s
Psychological Solutions 35

The 1960s
Marlene's Model 59

The 1970s
Career Moms 73

The 1980s
A Substitute Lover 93

The 1990s
Senior Serenade 105

Preface

This book presents stories of women's experiences and their changing roles from the 1930s through the 1990s. From teenagers through senior citizens, society's expectations for the female gender have changed with each ensuing decade. What was acceptable behavior at one period was taboo in another. In recent years, prohibitions were relaxed and greater freedom led to new ways for women to relate to each other.

In the nineteenth century, "romantic friendships" between women were not uncommon. Numerous accounts have been told of love affairs between women who were highly respected in their communities. Because of the taboos on premarital sex with men, a close relationship with another woman was condoned, since it was believed that it kept a woman "pure" and better prepared her for marriage. (Faderman, 1981, p. 75 ff) As women became more independent and assertive, attitudes regarding their social and sexual roles in their culture varied. Much of the changes were reflective of the political, economic and social trends of the times. *Ideas about what sexuality is and what forms of it are 'normal' change considerably over time **within cultures** and show marked variations **between cultures.***

(Howells, 1984, p. 2)

The women's movement in the sixties was an attempt to gain equal rights for women in the job market, but it also established a female identity among women which encouraged "sistership" and accepted lesbian relationships. The women described in the following stories were not essentially part of that movement, but its repercussions affected their lives and their attitudes. Although they had strong feelings for women, they did not consider themselves lesbians. Many were married and had good relationships with their husbands. However, an intimacy with another woman often led to desire for physical contact and to sexual fantasies.

As they became more independent and assertive, women's relationships with other women began to be viewed with increasing suspicion by society as a whole. Many men found the independent career woman to be a threat in the job market. Men became aware of the diminishing respect for a patriarchal culture which feminism promoted. With a passage of time and differences in the social climate, some men began to accept equality of women and began to assume roles and responsibilities previously relegated only to women. These changes in gender roles and in attitudes tended to bring women closer together to share many aspects of their experiences.

The stories in the following chapters exemplify aspects of women's roles which reflect changes in the social attitudes of their times. They are not reports of any specific research study, but are mainly incidents that have actually occurred. East story is followed by a commentary, based upon available literature, about the problems resulting from these real-life events.

I am grateful to those who have shared experiences with me. For obvious reasons, their names and the actual circumstances under which these incidents took place have not been revealed. Johnnye C. Bradley has been most helpful with the production of this work.

The stories are told in sequential order, beginning with teenagers in the 1930s and ending with senior citizens in a nursing home in the 1990s. Chapter One introduces the reader to two fourteen-year-olds experiencing the phenomenon of "teenage crush." The comments which follow describe the problems of identity in the adolescent years and the relationship of developing sexuality to that evolving identity.

Chapter Two is concerned with women in the military during the war years of the 1940s. Central to the story is the experience of a young WAC officer who had difficulty relating to both men and women at the Army camp. The comments discuss army regulations which caused the social isolation of the young officer. She solved her problem by establishing a close relationship with another female officer, and ultimately becoming involved with a civilian man.

In Chapter Three a student studying psychology became suspicious that her friend was too involved with another woman. She recommended that her friend see a psychiatrist. The 1950s were a time when psychoanalysis became popular, and psychiatric terms became part of the vernacular. It was also a time for conformity, when deviations in political outlook or in social relationships were ostracized. The discussion of this story concerns theories of homosexuality and comments as to the "normalcy" of various types of relationships.

In Chapter Four a photographer becomes emotionally involved with her model. Women's relationships with other women became intensified as they worked together in the women's movement of the 1960s and in job-related associations. The comments reflect back to the period of "romantic friendships" when this kind of relationship was acceptable.

In Chapter Five, the effects of the women's movement are more explicitly described as the reader becomes acquainted with three women who are trying to balance the responsibilities of motherhood with the demands of active careers. The comments include a brief review of the women's movement of the sixties and how it affected women's expectations in the seventies. The problems of "career moms" are discussed and some corroborating facts and information are presented.

The story in Chapter Six tells of a divorcee who was friendly with a married couple. When the husband died, the two women became more deeply involved. The friendship ended abruptly for no apparent reason. The discussion following the story of "Substitute Lover" deals with homophobia. Considered by many to be an "irrational" fear of homosexuals, it is both an excuse for avoidance of gays and lesbians and a defense mechanism used to protect the ego of the individual. Several authorities are cited to substantiate these claims.

The final chapter, Senior Serenade, deals with two elderly women in a nursing home. They share feelings and find common interests. The affectionate relationship that develops is beneficial to both of them. The comments discuss changing sexual orientation at various stages of life, the common problem of loneliness in old age, and reports of research studies of aging lesbians.

Hopefully, these examples of women's changing roles and the subsequent problems that evolved will offer reassurance to those readers who have had similar experiences, and will help others to understand the puzzling profusion of kinds of sexual identity in today's world.

REFERENCES

Faderman, Lillian. *Surpassing the Love of Men*. New York: William Morrow and Co., Inc., 1981.

Howells, Kevin ed. *The Psychology of Sexual Diversity*. New York: Basil Blackwell, Inc., 432 Park Ave. South, Suite 1505, NY 10016, 1984.

ONE

The 1930s

Teenage Crush

"Hi, I knew I would find you here." Sally approached Jean as she lay sprawled across the grass of the infirmary lawn. The girls had agreed to meet here whenever they could. Jean had asthma and had to come to the infirmary every afternoon for treatment. Sally had sprained her ankle playing tennis. Although it was better, she came to have it bandaged every other day.

Jean greeted Sally as she came along, "I have been waiting quite a while. Rest hour is almost over. We have to be getting back to our bunk." Jean and Sally were in the fourteen-year-old senior group at Camp Omega. Although they were not required to take naps during rest hour, they were to stay in their bunks and remain quietly on their beds. Both girls enjoyed getting out on one excuse or another, and the longer they could extend their outing the better they liked it.

Sally sat down on the grass near her friend. "Isn't it a lovely day? You can see the reflection of the trees and mountains on the lake. Naw, we don't have to go yet. The whistle won't blow for another half hour."

Sally seemed always ready to take risks, while Jean preferred to "play it safe" and not take a chance on getting caught. But now Jean leaned toward her friend and whispered, "She should be coming along soon, shouldn't she?"

Bobbi, the swimming counselor, would be coming along the path next to the infirmary lawn on her way to the lake. The girls liked to watch her vigorous stride, head held high, pony tail bouncing as she walked.

Sally looked squarely at her friend, as she confided, "Do you know she helped me to dive yesterday? She put her hand right on my back and made me lean forward a little."

"You lucky thing! Did you talk to her at all?"

"No, not really, but my leg brushed against hers. Her skin was so warm and the muscles so hard!"

Jean sighed, "If only I could touch her. I think about it every night before I go to sleep — and sometimes my pajamas get wet. Isn't that funny?"

"That happens to me sometimes too — when I think about Alexandria. You know, Mrs. Coleman. I told you about her."

"Tell me again. What doe she look like?"

"Well," Sally replied, "She is older than Bobbi, maybe twenty-five or twenty-six, or maybe even thirty. She has been teaching junior high for several years. She has blond hair and she pulls it back in a bun at the back of her neck. Sometimes she lets it loose and ties it with a ribbon. She looks younger that way. She smiles a lot and her teeth are very white — and her nose crinkles up when she smiles. But she can be strict sometimes too — if some kids are talking and not doing their work. She only has to look at one of us and we sit up and pay attention. Her eyes stare at us and she doesn't say a word."

"What does she teach?" Jean asked.

"Biology, but she doesn't always follow the book. She is very interested in the lady explorer — anthropologist, I think she is. Her name is Asa Johnson, and Mrs. Coleman would like to do what she does — go off to Africa and dig things up. Wouldn't that be exciting?"

"I don't know. It must be hot out there in the desert." Jean always saw the practical side of things.

"You sound like my mother — no sense of adventure. One day my mother came to school. It was Open School Night. She spoke to Mrs. Coleman. Do you know what my mother told her?"

"What?" Jean's eyes widened as she looked at her friend.

"She told Mrs. Coleman that I had a crush on her. And there we were right in the hall with other kids and mothers walking by. I could have died! I was so embarrassed!"

Jean's saucer eyes stared at her friend. "Golly, how awful! Why did your mother do that? What did you do? "

"I don't know. I think I ran down the hall. I couldn't talk to Mrs. Coleman for weeks after that, and I used to be a good student in her class. I was so mad at my mother. Mrs. Coleman was nice to me, but I always looked away when she talked to me. Finally, one day she met me on the playground when I was shooting baskets. She said she liked to play basketball too when she was in school. And she made me look at her. She said she hoped we were still good friends and she showed me a picture of her husband. Wasn't that nice of her?"

"Do you still think about her?"

"Yes, but I think about other people too. Look! Here comes Bobbi."

"She is wearing her new bathing suit. It is such a bright color blue — just like her eyes," Jean said. The girls lay on their stomachs with arms supporting their heads, facing the roadway leading to the lake. "Do you think she will notice us?"

Bobbi was walking her brisk, bouncy walk as she came down the path to the lake. Suddenly she stopped and took something out of her carrying bag.

Sally was quick to notice. "Look, she is taking something out of her bag. It's a cigarette. Did you know she smoked? I know the counselors are not supposed to smoke when they are with the kids. Do you suppose it's okay for her to smoke now?"

"I won't tell," Jean said. "Look at how she blows out the smoke — just like a movie actress." Bobbi was leaning against a tree, facing away from the road. She gazed off into the distance toward the mountains across the lake. Her classic profile, her well-proportioned body, her strong, shapely legs did, indeed, make her resemble a movie star.

"Did you see the movie, 'It Happened One Night?'" Sally asked.

"Yes, it was great! My mother didn't want me to see it at first because Clark Gable and Claudette Colbert slept in the same room and they weren't married," Jean responded.

"But they put up that sheet between them, remember?" Sally was surprised that Jean's mother would object.

"I know. They called it 'The Walls of Jericho,' like the story in the Bible. Did you like Clark Gable?" Jean asked.

"Yes, but I liked Claudette Colbert better. She was so cute when she pulled up her skirt to try to stop a car to give them a lift. Look at Bobbi. I bet she could stop some cars, too. What do you think she is thinking about?"

Bobbi was still leaning against the tree. One of her shapely legs was extended in front of her. She was still staring into space.

"I don't know," Jean answered. "Maybe about her boyfriend. The boys' camp is visiting this weekend and her boyfriend is a counselor there."

"Phewee! Who cares about boys?" Sally exclaimed.

"You will someday. My mother says that we don't like boys because we are not ready." Jean spoke with authority.

Sally screwed up her face. "I'll never be ready! Boys are uggish."

"Here comes Bobbi," Jean said. "We'd better look the other way or she'll see us staring at her."

Bobbi resumed her fast-paced walk toward the lake. "Hi, girls. See you later," she called.

"Isn't she great?" Jean asked. "She didn't even chase us or ask why we were here."

"Well, we'd better get going. Rest hour is nearly over." Sally's face lit up as she thought of an idea. "Let's take the road through the woods. Maybe we can find some salamanders along the way. Let's go that way."

It was a little longer and Jean resisted at first, but Sally was persistent. It had rained that morning and the salamanders would come out of their holes in the banks by the road when it rained. Each girl was able to find one. They picked up the little red newts by their tails and stroked their backs as they let them run across their hands.

"I'm going to keep mine in a tin can with moss in it. I'll keep it under my bed. And I can play with him and stroke his back every night. And I'm going to call mine 'Bobbi'," Jean said.

"I'll do that too. And I'll call mine Alexandria, after Mrs. Coleman." The girls headed back through the woods to their bunks, gently holding 'Bobbi' and 'Alexandria' by their tales.

The senior group of the boys' camp came to visit the next weekend. Since their campus was not nearby, they came by bus only twice a year.

"I don't know anyone at the boys' camp," Sally

commented to Jean. "It's silly to see them only twice a year. How can we get acquainted?"

"Well, they always have those 'mixer games' at the dance Saturday night," Jean responded. "Maybe you'll meet someone interesting."

Most of the senior girls were excited about the coming event. They were allowed to wear dresses or fancy pants suits which they had brought to camp for this occasion. They were also allowed to wear makeup. At fourteen, this was a special treat and there was much planning, chattering, and giggling among the girls as the date drew near.

When the girls arrived at the social hall, the boys were already there, sitting on benches along one wall of the room. They looked uncomfortable in their suits with jackets. They watched the girls as they came in and some leaned over to whisper something to the boys sitting next to them. The girls' camp head-counselor greeted the boys warmly, and then set down some rules.

"You are not to leave the social hall without telling your counselor. You are not to wander around the girls campus at any time. I am sure you will be polite to the young ladies. Have a good time!"

The boys' counselor then asked the boys to stand up and form a large circle. "Please do this quietly, without pushing or shoving," he warned. "Now the girls will make another circle outside of this one. No, you may not pick whom you want to stand next to! Just stand up where you are and follow Bobbi to make a circle outside the boys' circle."

"That must be Bobbi's boyfriend!" Jean whispered to Sally. "He knew her name and I could tell by the way he looks at her." She walked to a place in line and followed as the girls were led in a circle.

"Now, you will walk in time to the music, the girls going clockwise and the boys going counterclockwise. If you get mixed up, your counselors can help you. When the music stops, you are to face the boy or girl next to you and introduce yourself. My name is Doug and I'm going to get into the circle, too. Bobbi, will you get into the outside circle? Ready? Let's go!"

The pianist started to play and both boys and girls walked around the circle in different directions. Some took tiny steps, hesitating to see who was next to them. "Keep moving," Doug warned, "or you will have to sit down."

When the music stopped, Sally was standing next to a short, round-faced boy who came up to her shoulders. "Will I have to dance with him?" Sally thought. "He looks like a baby!" But she followed directions, introduced herself to the boy, whose name was Teddy, and proceeded to try to dance with him when the music started again. Teddy took small shuffling steps in a square. "Do you know the 'box step'?" he asked.

Sally nodded her head and tried her best to follow him.

"Would you like to get some punch?" Sally asked her partner after a while. Teddy looked relieved. The couple made their way over to the table with the punch and cookies.

Jean was there with a tall, thin boy named Sam. He was much bigger than Jean, but almost the same height as Sally.

"Do you mind if we change partners when the music starts again?" Sally asked.

"O.K." Jean responded. "Look at Bobbi and Doug. They still have their arms around each other, but the music has stopped!"

At that moment, Doug left Bobbi and went to the middle of the room "O.K., let's start again, guys, boys on the inside circle, girls on the outside, as you were before. Do not stand next to the partner you just had. We'll play the music again and when it stops you will introduce yourselves to someone new. O.K., Marty," he signaled the pianist to start to play.

"Begin walking, everybody."

After repeating this "mixer game" a few times, Doug announced that the boys may pick any partner they liked. "You may sit out this dance if you want to. This is a chance to talk to one another and to get acquainted."

"Are you going to sit with Sam?" Jean asked.

"He didn't ask me." Sally responded. "Besides, I'd rather watch the others."

The two girls sat down on the bench away from the piano so they could talk. "Watch Bobbi dancing with Doug," Jean said. "Look at the way she looks up into his eyes."

"They must really be in love," Sally smiled dreamily. "Do you think we will ever feel that way about a boy?"

The boys had brought sleeping bags with them and they were able to spend the night in the social hall after the dance. The following day a softball game was planned. The counselors set up the teams, dividing the boys and girls evenly and putting some good players to each side.

In the morning, teams were assigned and each met in a separate part of the mess hall after breakfast. Sally and Jean were on separate teams, but Sam was on the same team with Sally and Teddy was on Jean's team. They finally found things to say to each other.

"What position do you play?" Sally asked Sam.

"I'm usually an outfielder, and I'm pretty good at catching flies if there are any. What about you?"

"I like to pitch," Sally replied. "I don't know if the boys on the team will let me do that."

"They will if you're good enough. Let's get a ball and we'll go outside and practice."

Sam was elected captain of his team which they named "The Lakers". Sally was permitted to be the opening pitcher. Jean's team was called "The Sliders" since several of the boys knew how to slide into base.

The game was a close match, but the Sliders won as Teddy was able to slide safely into home base when Jean hit a double. "Wow, I couldn't have done that if you hadn't had such a good hit!" Teddy said to Jean. "And it went straight out to right field, so I was free to leave third base."

"You were really fast, Teddy, and it's great the way you can slide to the plate." Jean was genuinely impressed.

"Congratulations!" Sally said as she approached Teddy and Jean at the water fountain. "We didn't win," Sam said as he joined them. "But Sally pitched a pretty cool game, especially the first few innings."

It was time for the boys to board the bus to return to their own campus. As the girls stood by waving, Sam called to Sally, "I'll look for you next month when we come back."

"Yeah, me too," Teddy shouted, looking at Jean.

"It wasn't so bad," Sally told her friend after the bus left.

"See, I told you; those guys were really nice once they got started talking to us."

"I guess we'll get used to being with boys when we get back to school." Sally and Jean strode off toward their bunk with their arms around each other's shoulders.

COMMENTS

The phenomenon of teenage crush is common among adolescents. It is one process which helps the young person discover who he or she is. Defining one's identity often means leaving behind a part of one's self, taking on a new self and integrating the past and present selves — a task so difficult that Erik Erickson called it an "identity crisis".

Leaving the attachment to parents behind, adolescents tend to form new attachments to individuals of the same sex slightly older than themselves. Boys admire football and baseball stars, and collect autographs and pictures. Girls generally are attracted to teachers, counselors or baby sitters. Usually these infatuations are for young women whom the teenager admires and respects.

Perhaps these "crushes" are an intermediate stage between childhood and adulthood. Leaving childhood dependency upon a parent, the adolescent seeks someone to emulate. This is a means of "cutting loose" from parental ties, and is an important part of the developmental process. Parents complain that teenagers are assertive, independent and "won't listen to anything I say". The object of their devotion has shifted from the adult parent to another younger adult whom they can emulate. Sometimes sexual arousal is a component of this admiration. Sally and Jean each experience "wet dreams" connected with fantasies about the objects of their affections. This does not mean that they are "homosexual." According to Freud, there are three stages of sexual development.

The first stage is autosexuality, when the child becomes aware of himself as a source of sexual pleasure and consciously experiments with masturbation. The age range for this behavior is roughly two years through seven years.

The second stage is generally homosexuality, that is, love of members of one's own sex. Between 8 and 14 children find a "best friend" who becomes very important. He or she dares to be intimate which may involve physical contact. Between ten and twelve, young people entering puberty feel a growing need for closeness. Admiration for a same-sex adult, without experiencing any physical contact, may also result in sexual fantasies, as can be seen with our teenagers' crushes.

Love for the opposite sex (heterosexuality) usually follows the homosexual stage but in some cases it does not. Some argue that it is as natural to stay at stage 2 as it is to go on to stage 3.

The girls described in our story are at the stage 2 level of sexual maturity. As Jean's mother has told her, "You are not ready to like boys." Being in an environment of an all-girls camp may postpone the switch to heterosexual love, but the "crush syndrome" (if I may call it that) is evident in many cultures in early adolescence.

The love of animals is often present during these years. Boys like to "rough house" with the family dog. Girls frequently get obsessed with horseback riding. They love these animals, stroke them, talk to them and hug them. It is possible that they also receive vaginal stimulation while riding them.

Of course, Sally and Jean have chosen a somewhat unusual animal on which to vent their affections. In a country setting, pets such as frogs, snakes or salamanders often become pets. For girls, this may be a manifestation of an awakening maternal instinct, where they feel too old for dolls and too young to have real babies.

Adolescence comes to girls earlier and is accompanied by marked physical growth and body changes. A vivid imagination often helps to stem the tide of the emotional turmoil that such changes may cause. Adults would do well to accept these fantasies. A sense of humor, without ridicule, might help the teenager to distinguish fantasy from reality.

REFERENCES

Darcey, John Steward. *Adolescents Today.* Santa Monica, Calif: Goodyear Publishing Co., 1979.

Donahue, Ph. *The Human Animal.* New York: Simon and Schuster, 1985.

Erickson, Erik. *Childhood and Society.* New York: Norton, 1951.

Gay, Peter. *The Freud Reader.* New York: Norton, 1989.

Matthews, W.H., ed. *Oscar, From A to Z.* New York: Bantam Doubleday, Dill, 1995.

Singer, June. *Androgyny.* Garden City, N.Y. Anchor Press/Doubleday, 1976.

TWO

The 1940s

G. I. Gals

"Lt. Nancy Woodfield reporting for duty, Sir."

"At ease, Lieutenant. This Harrisburg base is your first assignment, is that correct?"

"Yes, Sir." Nancy looked straight ahead and thought, "I hope he doesn't think I'm scared. I'm not going to let him know — even if I am! He looks like he's trying to be tough, but that's the Army. He is probably a nice man, but he won't let it show!"

Nancy was familiar with Army ways since she had just completed training at OCS at Fort Des Moines, where the first Women's Army Auxiliary Corps (WAAC) training program had taken place. She was a strong-minded young woman and she very much wanted to be an Army officer.

"I see you did quite well. You even got a commendation for outstanding performance. Umm. Well, you may find things a lot different here. We don't give awards for good behavior here. We expect it."

"Yes, Sir."

"The women in your command come from different backgrounds. Some have been brought up in luxury and are not used to sweeping the floor or doing their own laundry. Some come from rural areas where they never wore shoes. They have never been disciplined. It is up to you to make good soldiers of all of them."

"Yes, Sir." Nancy thought, "I guess if I can control those teenagers in Harlem, I can handle these young women! I know you have to be tough at first, but a little kidding around won't hurt."

When she was taking her master's at Columbia's Teachers College, she did her student teaching in Harlem. Discipline problems were easy for her.

"I hope you have read your Officer's Training Guide carefully. There is to be no fraternizing with soldiers — male or female. This is a long-standing Army tradition that applies to women officers as well as men. You may not have dinner with a private or a noncommissioned officer, even if he is your brother. Do you have any questions?"

"No, Sir." Nancy had to try hard not to appear shocked or surprised at this last bit of information. Although her brother, now a corporal, was not stationed at this base, he was planning to visit her on his upcoming furlough.

"You will eat in the officer's mess hall. The only other women you will see there are the nurse lieutenants. Your duties will be explained to you in greater detail by Captain O'Toole in the morning. You are dismissed."

Nancy saluted, did an about-face, and walked erectly through the door and down the hall.

Major Emory shook his head and smiled slightly. "Do we really expect this attractive young woman to behave like an Army officer?" he thought. Although she seemed to be trying, it appeared to the major that she was playing a little game, and he could not take her seriously.

Nancy's duties were to do morning exercises with the women and to instruct them in field activities that were a mainstay of their training program. She had been a high school physical education teacher, so these assignments presented no problem for her. She was also to be responsible for the condition of the barracks, and checking the appearance of the soldiers under her command each day.

Since there were no other women officers other than the nurses, she was not able to live in the officers' quarters which were inhabited only by men. The nurses were quartered in the infirmary. Nancy's cot was in one of the barracks, but a small partition was set up for her so that she was separated from the other women. There was also a small desk and a chair, and of course, her footlocker at the end of the cot.

On the very first day, she heard the women talking about her. Since they did not see her come in, they were not aware of her presence. Although her quarters were closed off by the partition with a door for entrance, the separations did not extend to the ceiling, so that it was easy to hear whatever was said in the barracks.

"She seems okay."

"She used to be a teacher. I'll bet she'll treat us like children."

"I like her uniform. It's nicer than ours."

"Do you think she has a boyfriend? Will he have to salute her?" Giggles followed this remark.

"Well, I hope she is nicer than those guys — the officers that greeted us. They were a bunch of sourpusses."

"Let's give her a chance, gals. We'll soon find out."

Nancy did not interrupt this conversation. She did not, as yet, know the women well enough to recognize their voices, so she could not identify who was speaking. Obviously, she would have to win them over, just as she had to do the first few days of school.

After a week or so, Nancy was able to assess who was going to do well, who could be demoralizing, and who were natural leaders. She appointed line leaders from this later group to check on uniforms and cleanliness every morning. They were not required to report to her unless the transgression persisted for three or more days.

Nancy got to know the privates in her platoon quite well after a while. There were about forty women under her command, divided into two squads of twenty each.

Corporal Margaret Schlesinger alternated with Nancy in giving some of the drills and was billeted in the other barracks, having a partitioned area like Nancy's. She had been in the Army for several years and felt she know a good deal more than her superior officer, Lt. Woodfield, who had gone to OCS. Corporal Schlesinger's manner was gruff and she was disliked by many of the privates. This did not help her generally hostile attitude toward Lt. Woodfield, whom most of the privates seemed to admire. Nancy had to be extremely tactful in her relationship with her noncommissioned officer.

Skip, a heavy-set mature woman, was a good athlete and performed well in field activities. She was good natured and very willing to help others who might be having difficulty learning new skills. Nancy called on her frequently to help out.

Clarise was tall and attractive. She looked like a model and had been a college queen before she enlisted. But Clarise, in spite of her looks, was unpretentious in her manner and wanted very much to be "one of the girls."

The young woman who attracted Nancy's attention the most was Dorothy, a girl from a Midwestern farm area for whom every new experience was exciting. Dorothy was fair skinned, with light brown, shoulder-length hair (she might have to have it cut shorter) and a sprinkle of freckles across the bridge of her nose. She listened so attentively every time directions were given that Nancy soon found that she would focus upon Dorothy's face as she talked to the group.

There were others whom Nancy noticed. Madeline and Corkie (short for Cordelia) were usually seen together and often were holding hands. Nancy had to warn them that such action was not in military tradition, and that they should be sure not to display any kind of affection in public.

The military ruling on such matters was ambivalent. At the beginning of the war, in 1941, the military had concerns about homosexual males. Any man who had what were called "homosexual tendencies" was subject to court martial. Although femininity in a male was looked on as suspect by military psychologists, masculinity in a female would not render her undesirable. As a matter of fact, many athletic women were attracted to the military. There were instances of homosexuality, but these were generally ignored. Since the need for personnel grew as the war progressed, the policy toward homosexuality became more lenient.

Nancy had little difficulty with problems related to homosexuality until she found herself personally involved with it.

One day she found a note on her bed:

Dear Lieutenant Woodfield,

I must tell you how much I admire you. You are always fair and so cheerful. I love your strong voice and the way you walk. I can't keep my eyes off you, and I think about you all the time.

I'd like to know more about you. What was it like in your home and what you did before you got into the Army. Could we meet sometime just to talk? If there is anything I could do for you, please tell me.

I would do anything.

With love,
Dorothy Vance

After reading the note carefully, Nancy knew exactly what Dorothy was experiencing. She, herself, had crushes on teachers and camp counselors when she was younger. She was fond of Dorothy and wanted more than anything not to hurt her feelings.

One morning, when Corporal Schlesinger was giving morning exercises, Nancy asked to have Private Vance excused for a short time so that she could speak to her alone.

Dorothy came to her room looking timid and afraid. Avoiding any military terms, Nancy said, "Sit down, Dorothy. I just want to talk to you for a minute."

Dorothy sat on the one available chair while Nancy sat at the edge of her cot. "Thank you so much for your note and the nice things you said about me."

"That wasn't half of it. I would like to say more." Dorothy blushed and cast her eyes down.

"You don't have to. I understand how you feel."

"You can't know," Dorothy protested. "I never felt this way before, about anybody!"

"But I have," Nancy assured her. "I had a crush on a teacher once. She was my major advisor in college and she seemed to understand me so well. We were able to talk once in a while and I used to go to her office whenever I had something on my mind that I needed to discuss. She helped me make up my mind about going into the Army, although I was out of college by then and she was no longer my advisor. She remained my friend."

"Can you be my friend?" Dorothy asked hopefully.

Nancy hesitated, "It would be hard right now. I am very fond of you, Dorothy, but the Army has certain rules. Officers cannot 'fraternize' with privates. They are very strict about this. I would get into trouble if I were seen socializing with you, even if it were just to have a cup of coffee in the day room."

"That's awful! You can't have any friends, because there are no other women officers around here." Dorothy was quick to see Nancy's side of the story.

"That's right. And I don't like it much. I can't date privates or noncoms either. The officers here are older and, if anything, they consider me an intruder. I do eat in their mess hall where there are a few women officers who are nurses. We have our meals together." Dorothy looked at her idol with pleading eyes. "But I really do love you, doesn't that make a difference?"

"Yes, it means a lot to me to hear you say that. I wish I could do something about it. Perhaps after your basic training is over and you are assigned some place else, we can keep in touch with each other. We can write to each other, and after the war is over, we can meet some place. But Dorothy, you are young and you will fall in love again. Perhaps you will meet a young man and eventually get married."

"I don't think I have ever liked boys much. There is a guy back home. He will have his own farm some day. My folks think he is just right for me."

"Don't you care for him?"

"He has been a friend. We used to ride the bus to school together. But I don't love him."

"Perhaps some day you will. But you will meet lots of new people while you're in the service. You share so many new experiences with each other. There are other women who would love to have you as a special friend. You are so fresh-looking and lovely, and such a sweet, caring person." Nancy reached out and took Dorothy's hand gently in her own. "We won't talk about this again, but I will not forget you. Go back with your squad now. You are dismissed, Private Vance."

There were tears in Dorothy's eyes as she stood up, saluted, and left the barracks.

Nancy thought about Dorothy a good deal in the next few weeks. She tried hard not pay any special attention to her, but occasionally their eyes met and she was able to give her a reassuring look.

It was difficult having no one to talk to. Nancy was an outgoing person who enjoyed sharing her experiences with others. Talking on any personal level to the women in her platoon was not condoned. The male officers either were amused by her or were hostile to her. Even though she was respected by some for doing a good job, there was a constant, all pervasive awareness that women had invaded a male preserve.

"Hey, here comes the Petticoat Army!" a group of soldiers shouted as the WAAC platoon marched by. The women ignored these comments and kept their eyes focused straight ahead. But later, several of them came to Nancy with complaints. They got remarks like this whenever they crossed the campus. It was easy to take when they were involved in routines, but alone or in pairs in the PX or on days off in town, they found this harassment very disturbing.

Nancy decided to go to her commanding officer to discuss this. She approached Captain O'Toole one morning in his office.

"Sir," she began. "The women are complaining that they get insulting remarks from male soldiers both on and off the base. After all, we are serving in the armed forces just as they are, and we deserve a little respect."

"I'm sorry, Lieutenant," Captain O'Toole replied. "There is nothing I can do about that. When the men are off duty, I have no control of the situation."

"But can't you speak with them some time and let them know how offensive this behavior is?"

"I told you there is nothing I can do about it." Captain O'Toole's voice was stern.

Nancy left the office with some disappointment. She knew she could not go to Major Emory. It was Army policy not to go over the head of the next in command, and although Major Emory might be more sympathetic, he would not welcome her attempt to override Captain O'Toole's decision.

Nancy tried to explain this to her platoon. "If women in the military are not taken seriously, it is not only here that we do not get equal treatment. Careers for women have never been condoned. Perhaps things will be better after the war. I hope we will have made a difference."

"But what can we do about it now?" Skip asked.

"We can ignore it as much as possible," Nancy replied. "But when we are off duty, we might try a little teasing ourselves."

"What do you mean, Lieutenant?" Skip asked.

"Well, you might pick out the men who are the worst offenders and find some names to call them. They might be fat or bald or whatever. When you are in the barracks some time you might try to think up some appropriate nicknames. If they fit, the other guys will soon pick up on them."

"That's a great idea. You are a good sport, Lieutenant Woodfield," Clarise chimed in.

"Will you help us think up some names?" Dorothy asked.

"Oh, no," Nancy answered quickly. "and I don't want you to tell anyone that I suggested this, either."

As the weeks went by, Nancy found that she looked forward to her meals with the nurses in the officer's mess hall. One lieutenant in particular, Claudia Hollaway, seemed interested in her experiences with her WAACs. When she was not on duty evenings, Nancy went back to Claudia's room in the infirmary. Sometimes they played cards, sometimes they watched television in the day room.

Claudia was a widow who had lost her husband, a pilot, who had been shot down in a mission over Berlin. They had been married only a short time and had no children. Claudia had not talked about her loss to anyone. Somehow she liked to tell her new friend about her handsome young husband and the good times they had together when he was stationed at a nearby base.

One evening when Nancy had gone back to Claudia's room, they stretched out on her cot looking at pictures of Claudia and her husband at a state fair. They were riding on the cyclone and Claudia's head was buried on his shoulder.

"I was so afraid riding on that thing!" Claudia said. "A friend took our picture just as we were coming down. Jim was never afraid of heights or of fast-moving rides. That's why he enjoyed being a pilot, I guess." There were tears in Claudia's eyes as she talked about this. Nancy reached out and took her hand. Claudia leaned toward her and put her head on Nancy's shoulder. She sobbed briefly and then said, "I'm sorry. I don't often break down like that."

Intimacy between the two women continued to grow. Soon they found that they enjoyed spending nights together, and Nancy remained with Claudia until morning. A sexual relationship developed. Neither of them had experiences like this before, but somehow they knew what to do, how to please each other.

There were other women on the base who had relationships with women. When Nancy returned to her barracks at daybreak she often found Madeline and Corkie asleep in the same narrow cot. And there were others. Everyone knew about them but no one spoke of it. The word "lesbian" was never used. Claudia and Nancy were happy together, but there was so much that could not be expressed because of the enforced silence about these relationships.

Some men had also coupled off, but they had to hide their feelings even more than the women. The nurses seemed to know, but did not discuss it except among themselves. They seemed to recognize that Army life was difficult and soldiers were lonely. If the officers knew about these relationships, nothing was said. Men could be court-martialed for being gay. Displays of affection between women were not condoned, but no disciplinary action was taken. Nancy had been asked by Captain O'Toole, her immediate commanding officer, to talk with Madeline and Corkie about any overt display of affection. Nancy did that with as much tact as she could muster. Fortunately, male officers never patrolled WAAC barracks.

Things went smoothly for Lieutenant Woodfield and her platoon for the remainder of the training period. All of the women in her division were to pass their task-oriented examination at the end of the twelve-week period, and were to be reassigned to their bases.

Nancy was also to be reassigned, although she was still to remain in Harrisburg. An intensive recruitment campaign was being planned. Officers who had rejected the idea of having women working in their departments were now requesting them. The initial enthusiasm to join the WAACs when doors were first opened to women in 1942 had diminished by 1944 as the demands grew. Nancy was notified to report to Major Emory's office one morning shortly before the final week of the training program.

"Lieutenant Woodfield, I have good news for you. You will be reassigned to the recruiting office and will live in town for the next few months. The Army needs more women and it is felt that a woman officer doing recruiting will attract more of the high quality women we want. You will be interviewing men as well as women. You will be promoted to the rank of Captain. Congratulations!"

"Thank you, Sir." Nancy was startled and somewhat pleased about this new assignment. She certainly did not expect a promotion so soon. She would miss her evenings with Claudia, but Nancy was always excited about new experiences. Her job on the base had become quite routine. "But who will be doing the training program, Sir?" Nancy asked.

"A new lieutenant will be sent here from the OCS at Ft. Des Moines. You might be required to remain here for awhile to help her get started. And, of course, Captain O'Toole is still in charge of the training program."

"You will be given funds to rent a room in town, and you may return to the base whenever you are not on duty and can find transportation. I know you will give this position your best effort. Good luck, CAPTAIN." Major Emory stressed the name of her new rank, and seemed to be pleased about her promotion.

It was while Nancy was working in the recruiting office she met Tony Santoro. He came to her desk, passing by two male recruiting officers and asked, "Can I sign up here?"

"You can fill out some forms and apply here," Nancy responded. "You will be called for your physical within a week."

In filling out his application, Nancy found out a good deal about Anthony Santoro. He was twenty-four years old and single. He lived with his parents who ran a small grocery store and vegetable market in a working class neighborhood of Harrisburg. He had one sister who was planning to become a nun after she finished high school. He was the only son and his parents depended upon him to help them run the business.

"If your parents need you, why do you want to sign up for the Army now?" Lieutenant Woodfield asked.

"My draft number will come up soon, but I thought I'd have a better chance to choose what I'd like to do if I volunteered."

"What would you want to do?"

"I'd like to be trained as a radio technician or in something that has to do with communication. I put together my own crystal set when I was a kid." Tony spoke with a good deal of confidence, but there was a slight foreign intonation in his speech.

"What language is spoken in your home?" Nancy asked.

"Italian. My folks don't speak much English. How did you know? Don't I speak good English?"

"Yes, you do, Mr. Santoro," Nancy was quick to answer. "It's your name and the way you spoke about your family. Italians seem to me to be such devoted family members."

Tony smiled, showing a row of strong, white teeth, "Yeah, we all like each other. I have lots of aunts, uncles and cousins, too. Some of them have been in this country longer than my folks."

"What do you do now? Are you going to school?"

"I work in my father's store. I finished high school and I've started to take some college courses at night. This term I am taking accounting."

"That sounds fine. Just sign here and I will process your application. You will hear from us about your physical next week."

Tony got up and bowed slightly. "Am I supposed to salute you? I see you are a captain."

"No, not yet. You can wait until you are a soldier!" Nancy smiled as she dismissed him. "Good luck!"

It was two weeks later that she saw Tony again. This time he looked very depressed.

"Captain Woodfield, I didn't pass my physical. I have a sinus condition and I have allergies. I've had that all my life. I didn't think that would keep me from joining the Army!"

"That is the decision of the medical staff, Mr. Santoro. I cannot do anything about it. I'm sorry."

"Will my draft number come up anyway?"

"No, probably not. The results of your physical will go on your record."

"But I really want to be in service. I want to help with the war effort."

"There are lots of ways you can help as a volunteer. You can work in the veterans' hospital. I even think we use some volunteers in this office. I will inquire about it. Possibly you could do some filing one or two evenings a week."

It was in this way that Nancy and Tony got to know each other. Tony came into the office three nights a week, that is, every night he did not go to night school. Nancy usually had work to do and she arranged to do it on the nights that Tony was there. Since he was a civilian, he was permitted to call Nancy by her first name. Often they went out for coffee after the office was closed. For the first time since she came to Harrisburg, Nancy found someone to laugh with. Tony had a great sense of humor and told stories about the people who came into his family's store. Many of them tried to bargain with him. He knew who they were and always quoted a higher price for them so that he could come down a little at their pleading.

Nancy and Tony continued to see each other. Occasionally they went to a movie or dancing at a small cafe in Tony's home neighborhood. They tried to avoid places frequented by the military from the base. Nancy had checked the Officer's Guide Book but had found nothing forbidding officers to be seen with civilians.

At a theater in downtown Harrisburg, far from the Army base, Nancy and Tony saw "Casablanca", a movie they would never forget. It had been nominated for an Academy Award, and everyone was talking about it. Humphrey Bogart and Ingrid Bergman were the most romantic couple to have hit the screen.

"You know, we really do have men stationed in Casablanca," Tony remarked. "Just last spring, American and British forces began a drive against the Germans in Morocco. Paul Henried played the part of one of those Allied agents. I guess he needed Bergman's support to carry out his mission."

"I don't know if I'd give up Bogie for that stuffy agent character!" Nancy said.

"You know," Tony sounded prophetic, "that picture will be remembered long after the Allies' drive in Morocco is forgotten!"

After Nancy had been in service eighteen months, she was entitled to a leave of absence. She planned to go back to her parents' home in Skokie, a suburb of Chicago.

She told Tony about her leave, saying she might be gone several weeks.

"How can I get along without you that long, Babe?" His nickname for Nancy seemed to give him more confidence in dealing with an Army officer. Nancy liked it. Everyone else she knew treated her with respect or indifference. She remembered that her father, whom she adored, used to call her "Babe" when she was little. It's strange that Tony picked that pet name, without knowing anything about her father's use of it.

"Why don't you come with me?" Nancy asked.

Tony flushed with excitement. "I don't know anything about Skokie, Illinois. I've never been outside of Harrisburg!"

"Then it's about time you were. I'd like you to meet my family."

"What would they think of me? I never went to college. My folks are poor. They don't even speak English."

"But you do. You were born in this country and you're an American. My grandparents were born in Germany, and now we are fighting the Germans. My father sends money to try to get some of his family out of the concentration camps."

"Does that mean you are Jewish? I didn't know that. My folks are very upset about what's happening to the Jews in Germany. They didn't like it when Mussolini joined up with Hitler, either."

"I've met your folks, Tony, and they are very nice people. I'd like you to meet mine."

She sent the following letter to tell her folks of her plans:

Dear Mom and Dad,

At last I will be getting some time off and I will be coming home to see you. I am really looking forward to being with you soon.

I want to tell you that I will be bringing a young man with me whom I want you to meet. He is Antonio Santoro and he lives here in Harrisburg. His folks run a grocery store here and he helps them out working in the store. But Tony has other plans. He is going to college at night and is studying accounting. He is very ambitious and he has the ability to go far.

I know we come from different backgrounds. He is Catholic and his folks were born in Italy. I hope you will be able to accept these differences because I love Tony and think I would like to spend the rest of my life with him. Above all else, he is a compassionate person and he cares a great deal for me.

I think he will care about you too, and you will love him when you get to know him.

I would like to have been able to tell you this in person, but there was not time to do so. Telephone calls are not very private here, so I had to do this in writing. Please understand.

Your loving daughter,
Nancy

Nancy was able to arrange a leave for the Thanksgiving holiday. The Woodfields were cordial to Tony when he arrived in Skokie. They had been prepared by Nancy's letter, and although they had some misgivings, they respected their daughter's opinions. It wasn't long before they began to treat Tony as a member of the family. His hearty manner and his sense of humor made it easy for them to relate to him.

"Do you want some more turkey?" Mrs. Woodfield asked. "Help yourself, Tony."

"You sound just like my mom," Tony said. "Mangiara bene, Tony! That's all I hear at my house. You'd think I'd be big and fat by now."

"You're getting there," Nancy patted his stomach. "I guess moms are all alike."

"Anyway, Jewish and Italian moms have that in common." Mr. Woodfield chipped in. "If you don't eat well at their dinner table, they get insulted!"

Mrs. Woodfield was watching the little playful gestures between Nancy and Tony. "When are you two going to announce the date?" She was concerned that this close relationship could lead to problems if the young people were not married.

"Uh--well. We haven't talked about that yet." Tony blushed and looked sideways at Nancy.

"Gee, Mom, give us a chance. There's a war going on and things are so uncertain. I could get transferred and Tony might meet someone else."

"Not on your life!" Tony responded quickly. "We'll get around to making plans, Mrs. Woodfield. Don't worry."

Nancy remained in Harrisburg for the duration of the war. Upon her discharge, she and Tony were married and went to live in Skokie near her parents' home.

Claudia Hollaway remained a good friend and came to visit the Santoro's quite often. She eventually married again and had a family. Although she lived in Boston, the two families managed to spend holidays together, taking the children sight-seeing to historic places in both of their home towns.

In 1995, when there was a ground breaking ceremony for a memorial to honor women in service, both families met in Washington. Like military people throughout the country, Nancy and Claudia enjoyed reminiscing about their days in the military in Harrisburg.

COMMENTS

The war offered many opportunities for women to develop relationships with other women. The novel excitement of working with competent, independent women plus the absence of frequent contact with men made the women's services a unique experience. For those who already identified themselves as lesbians, joining the WAACs, the WAVEs or the Women Marine Corps seemed a logical decision. For others who had not identified themselves in such a way, the military provided a new emotional stimulus and they were frequently drawn to some woman with whom they worked.

Dorothy's deep attraction to Lieutenant Nancy Woodfield is very understandable. Coming from a farm area in the middle west, she probably knew strong women who worked hard, but none of them would be in positions of authority. The admiration she felt for Nancy seemed natural to her. It is very likely that she never heard of "lesbianism", but she was strong enough to have left her secure, rural lifestyle to seek something different for herself. Thus, she had few restraints about trying new directions and different experiences. Her openness and naivete were appealing to Nancy.

It was not that homosexualism was forbidden, but the relationship of a commissioned officer to a private that was not allowed. Nancy missed companionship and eventually found a satisfying relationship with a fellow officer, the nurse, Claudia Hollaway.

The following incident was told by a World War II WAC sergeant, in an interview years later (Faderman, 1991, p. 118):

"Yes, Sir. If the General pleases I will be happy

> *to do this investigation ... but, Sir, it would be unfair of me not to tell you, my name is going to head the list ... You should also be aware that you are going to have to replace the file clerks, the section heads, most of the commanders, and the motor pool ... I think you should also take into consideration that there have been no illegal pregnancies, no cases of venereal disease, and the General himself has been the one to award good conduct commendations and service commendations to these members of the WAC detachment."*

General Eisenhower: "Forget the order." (Bunny MacCulloch interview with Johnnie Phelps, 1982)

It can be seen that sexual experiences that may be socially acceptable during one era may be considered sick, dangerous or antisocial during another. Economic or practical matters (such as the need for women to perform necessary jobs in military service during war time) determine the shift in attitudes in brief spaces of time.

Nancy and Claudia's relationship was dependent upon the time period in which it took place. Neither of these women was homosexual, although they enjoyed homosexual experiences. No doubt this is true in prisons, hospitals, and other places where sexes are cut off from each other. Various reports from women's colleges such as Vassar and Bryn Mawr provide evidence of such incidents.

So although women's relationships with other women were not condoned, they were, to some extent, overlooked. Men on the base still teased WACs with name calling like "Petticoat Army", or "Amazons". Recruitment of women became, as time went on, more difficult. The negative attitude of G.I.s was one of the factors that brought the recruiting campaign to slow halt. Also, industry had begun to offer high-paying jobs to women. And other military services seemed to offer more advantages, (e.g. nicer uniforms) than the WAACs. The organization and physiology of the Army recruiters seemed to be obstacles, we well. (Holm, 1982, pp. 47-8)

At the same time, commanding officers began to admit that the services of women were of great value. A study concluded that "economical, efficient, and spirited results are achieved in military installations where both male and female personnel are on duty". (Holm, 1982, p. 101) Because of the growing importance of women's role in the military, and because of manpower shortages in 1943 and 1944, a reorganized recruitment drive was initiated.

In the late summer of 1943, the Woman's Auxiliary Army Corps became the Woman's Army Corps, and the WAC was integrated into the regular Army company channels. Army women were entitled to equal pay and benefits normal to military status. In addition, women officers could command men as well as women, and could be employed in various divisions of the service previously closed to them.

Probably as a result of this reorganization, Lieutenant Nancy Woodfield was placed in the recruitment office and was raised to the rank of captain. Although the promotion was welcomed, the change of responsibilities presented additional problems of social isolation.

Recruiting officers were expected to live in town, rather than in a dormitory or barracks. For women in service, the dormitory served as a refuge from the whole gamut of sexual harassment that they were customarily subject to. It was one place where women could retreat from outside pressures. Women often used their money to fix up dormitories or barracks with drapes, furniture and equipment to make coffee or snacks. They felt conspicuous at most recreational activities at the base which were basically designed to accommodate the interests of men.

One female corporal complained, "You can't even go into the chow hall without running the gauntlet. You feel naked and you want to hide ... You can't complain to the women officers because they are powerless to do anything about it. Besides, they get the same hassle from the guys — sometimes worse." (Holm, 1982, p. 76)

The dating situation for a female officer was very restrictive. "Any female line officer who socialized with enlisted men was considered to be a traitor to her class; but interestingly, a nurse was not. Moreover, the burden of complying with the rule was placed mainly on the woman in each case. If caught in the act of fraternizing, it was she who was disciplined, rarely the man." (Holm, 1982, p. 74)

It is little wonder that women officers had to seek unusual forms of companionship during the time of services.

REFERENCES

Blacksmith, E.A. *Women in the Military*. New York: Wilson, 1992.

Faderman, Lillian. *Odd Girls and Twilight Lovers*. New York: Columbia University Press, 1991.

Holm, Jeanne. *Women in the Military*. Novato, CA: Presidio Press, 1992.

Humphrey, Mary Ann. *My Country, My Right to Serve*. New York: Harper Collins, 1990.

Marrs, T.W. *Every Woman's Guide to Military Service*. Cockeyville, Md.: Liberty Publications, 1989.

Schneider, Dorothy and Carl J. Schneider. *Sound Off*. New York: Dutton, 1988.

Slappey, Mary McG. *Exploring Military Service For Women*. New York: Rosen Publishing Group, 1989.

Stiehm, Judith. *Arms and the Enlisted Woman*. Philadelphia, Pa.: Temple University Press, 1989.

THREE

The 1950s

Psychological Solutions

Gail and Barbara had been close friends at Brooklyn College where both majored in psychology. In the 1940s when they were students, many eventful things were happening. A new campus in Flatbush, a suburban area of Brooklyn, had just been opened after years when classes had been held in office buildings downtown. The newly-formed psychology department was staffed with young professors who had recently completed their doctorates. They had been taught by outstanding scholars who had left Germany due to the rise of Hitler. New ideas, from Freudian adherents to the avant-guard thinking of Gestalt psychology, flooded the college classrooms. Young, bright psychology majors were fascinated by the wealth of ideas to which they were exposed.

In one of Barbara's classes she was asked to help with a survey using a questionnaire to determine the self-concept of the individuals interviewed. She tried this out on her friend, Gail, who objected to this methodology.

"How can you determine how somebody feels about himself by asking him questions? You know that anyone with any sense will answer in ways that give a good impression," Gail reasoned.

"The questions are not that obvious," Barbara replied. "Dr. Moreley feels that if you are an independent thinker, you answer one way, but if you're a conformist you answer another. He is really trying to determine if the individual is controlled by his environment or is in control of it."

Barbara tried to get her boyfriend, Chuck, to answer the questionnaire but he refused. "He sounded just like you," Barbara reported to Gail. "He also thought that some of the questions were an invasion of privacy."

Chuck Isaacson was dating Barbara and Arnie Stevens was dating Gail. Neither of the men were taking psychology. Chuck thought the subject was just a lot of talk and not very scientific. He was a science major while Arnie was in social studies, with strong political interests. Marxism was frequently a topic of conversation. Arnie was active with the American Student Union chapter on campus. Gail and Barbara joined it also but were not always in full agreement with its policies. Chuck was busy with late laboratory periods and had no time for campus politics. The two couples remained friendly despite strong differences of opinions.

In their senior year at college, Japan attacked Pearl Harbor. Upon graduation, both men joined the armed forces, expecting to be drafted shortly. Gail and Barbara became teachers. Each of them kept in close touch with each other and with their boyfriends. Fortunately the men remained in the U.S. during the war. Chuck instructed in celestial navigation at an air base in Kansas. Arnie went to OCS and became a recruiting officer at Fort Dix. They were able to visit Barbara and Gail while on furlough or leave.

Both couples were married shortly after the end of the war. The men decided to use the allowance from the G.I. bill to go back to school for their Master's degrees. Barbara and Gail continued in the school system and became the main support of their husbands for the next two years.

The women spent a good deal of time with each other at this time. They frequently went to movies and had long discussions about the films that they saw.

"I don't know why they allow so much sex to be shown on the screen lately," Gail complained. "It sort of spoils it if nothing is left to the imagination."

"Yes," Barbara agreed. "Do you remember that picture 'Love is a Many Splendored Thing?' That was certainly mushy. Yet I read that it was the top box office film of the year!"

"That's what I mean," Gail agreed. "The best thing about it was the theme song. That won an award."

"People are more open about sex now than they used to be," Barbara responded knowingly. "There are even studies that show that homosexuality is more prevalent than we used to think."

"Why are you so interested in that?" Gail asked curiously. "Somehow we always end up talking about it."

"I guess it's because homosexuals have been more open. I think they have a right to exist without persecution like any other minority group. I just read that President Eisenhower banned the employment of homosexuals in government positions. That's not fair. They are not doing anything to hurt other people." Barbara sounded indignant.

"It's all because of McCarthy and his House Unamerican Activities Committee. Everyone has become suspicious of everyone else," Gail responded.

"Do you know that Chuck made me get rid of some books about Karl Marx that I had since college? We really had arguments about that," Barbara confessed sheepishly.

"Arnie is just the opposite. He feels that we should write letters to Congressmen protesting McCarthy's investigations." Gail shrugged her shoulders. "He thinks we should be out there in every protest rally. I'm not sure he isn't right."

"Chuck is afraid that we might have trouble with our jobs in the school system. You know some of our psych professors have been fired. Did you hear Edward R. Murrow last night? He accused McCarthy of telling half-truths and confusing the public about the internal dangers of communism."

"It's scary, isn't it?" Gail retorted. "Soon we'll be afraid to say anything that might sound suspicious."

"I know what you mean," Barbara agreed. "I am really sorry I let Chuck talk me into throwing out my books on Marxism. That's almost like the burning of books under the Nazis. And now I'm reading books about sex and homosexualism. I suppose those are considered suspect, too. Yet there are a lot more of them available now." Barbara looked quizzically at Gail, trying to read her reactions. However, nothing more was said on the subject at this time. Barbara had always felt a strong affection for Gail. She had shown outward signs of her feelings, but Gail had never been very responsive.

"What about war pictures?" Gail was quick to change the subject. "'From Here to Eternity' got eight Academy Awards this year. It really was about how cruel men were to each other when they were in service."

"But it also showed how much some men cared for each other. Maggio, the Frank Sinatra character and Pruett, who was played by Montgomery Clift, were certainly more than just friends."

"Sinatra got the award for best supporting actor," Gail

shifted the subject again. "Would you ever imagine that the singer that all the girls swooned over when we were kids would turn into a fine serious actor?"

"I never 'swooned' over him," Barbara responded quickly. "I never could see what all the other kids saw in him."

"Now there is a new heart-throb." Gail said. "His name is James Dean. Do you remember him in 'East of Eden'? He's not only sexy looking but he can act! His character, Cal, is so vulnerable. He's a nonconformist and life is difficult for him."

"I guess it was always hard to be different." Barbara sounded serious, as if she had been thinking about this for a long time. "That picture was supposed to happen before World War I, and people wanted conformity then. And they still do. If you think differently or have a different life style, you are likely to be investigated by the Unamerican Activities Committee!"

"It seems that some of the best people get investigated," Gail said. "Directors and actors in Hollywood, playwrights like Lillian Hellman, and even professors who teach psychology — not even politically involved people."

"You know," Barbara seemed to be continuing with the same train of thought. "In 'The Caine Mutiny' everyone got investigated. First, Captain Queeg came before a hearing and was removed from office. Then the young Lieutenant, the one played by Van Johnson, was brought up for court-martial. Captain Keefer, Fred MacMurray's character was the one who undermined Captain Queeg, but he let the Lieutenant take all the blame."

"Yes, it's hard to tell who the heroes are," Gail said. "It's not like it used to be with the old cowboy pictures. I think the movies today show the disillusionment of people. I wonder what makes a man like Captain Queeg act that way? He must have been neurotic to begin with."

Gail became more interested in pursuing the study of psychology as her concern for the political climate continued to deepen. Her former psychology professor, Dr. Moreley, no longer taught at Brooklyn College, but was now associated with the New School for Social Research in New York. Gail decided to take courses there. At first she simply wanted to know more about current research, but eventually she decided to continue toward her Master's degree and try to become a school psychologist. She told Barbara, "It is good to be in a stimulating environment again, where students and teachers discuss ideas freely without apparent fear of repression."

Barbara also took classes after school. She began studying dance at the New Dance Group, a school formed by several modern dancers that was very popular among young working women. Barbara had always been interested in dance, but had not taken lessons since her childhood days. Modern dance was very different from the tap, acrobatic and ballet school she had attended as a child. It took her a while to adjust to the discipline and serious intent of the dancers she met.

One of the students, Polly Defoe, was a young black woman who had just graduated from Hunter College. She was very bright and her family had expected her to go on to medical school. Her interest in the dance took priority over that. She began taking several classes a week, while working in an office during the day time. She and Barbara were the newest members of the class and they became friends. They frequently went out for a bite to eat after class.

Polly wanted to perform and had developed a style of African dance that had not appeared on concert stages at this time. Without instruction in this type of movement, Polly seemed to instinctively move in patterns similar to tribal dances.

Barbara was the only person who encouraged Polly to pursue this direction in her dance compositions. The teachers at the New Dance Group were impressed with her strength and her ability to jump to great heights, but their attitudes were somewhat patronizing. "How amazing that Polly has such great elevation" or "She had little training but she may have a future," the staff members were heard to comment. No one seemed to understand Polly's drive and her intuitive feeling for her long-buried roots.

Her parents were not understanding either. They were Jamaican and had little identity with African culture. They were disappointed that Polly was not pursuing her earlier ambition to become a doctor.

"I really know that the dance is what I have to do," Polly confided to Barbara, as they sipped their cokes at the corner drugstore near the studio. "It's not even something I planned for myself. It just happened."

"Then you have to keep it up," Barbara said encouragingly, "If you need a place to practice, you can come to our apartment for a weekend if you like. We have an empty room that we never had the money to furnish. We can put a cot in there so you can sleep over if you want to."

"That would be great," Polly answered. "I could come after class on Saturday morning. Are you sure your husband won't mind?"

"He plays golf on Saturdays, and we usually go out for dinner in the evening. You'll have the whole place to yourself."

This arrangement worked out well. Polly came to Brooklyn several weekends and worked on her dances. When she wanted to show them and get some criticism, Polly invited Barbara to watch.

"That is really terrific!" Barbara said after viewing Polly's latest choreography. "No one has ever done things like that in New York. There's that dancer from Chicago I've heard about. Her name is Katherine Dunham, but she has studied anthropology. Where do you get your ideas from?"

"I really don't know. Kids in Harlem do some jiving on the streets, and who knows where they get it from?"

Sometimes Polly taught a movement to Barbara so that she could get the feeling of it better. Barbara was excited when they moved together and touched each other. She was fascinated with Polly's strong body, her intensity as she danced, her total concentration. After a long session, Polly would stretch out on the floor in a state of complete relaxation. Barbara enjoyed watching her. She lay down on the floor next to her, seeing Polly's breathing as it slowed down after the rapid pace which followed her strenuous movement.

"You know," Barbara said. "You should show these dances to someone. I think you are ready to perform."

"The gals at the New Dance Group don't think so. They think I am just a beginner."

"Oh, I don't mean them. They are too busy trying to advance their own careers. Why don't you try some nightclub or something like that?"

"I never thought of that!" Polly responded with a twinge of excitement. "I know a gal who performs in Greenwich Village. Maybe she has some contacts."

It was not long before Polly was dancing at a popular club in the Village. To her surprise, she was reviewed favorably by an important dance critic. After that, her career was launched. She made guest appearances and began to organize her own group. She continued to take classes at the New Dance Group, and still spent some Saturday afternoons at Barbara's apartment, practicing and choreographing. And Barbara continued to talk about her to Gail. "She is so talented, and unique. Nothing she does when she choreographs is like anything that we do in class. I don't know where her ideas come from."

"She might have seen it at home or at parties with her friends. After all, she is black and the things she does stem from her culture," Gail commented.

"No, her parents are Jamaican and have been in this country for quite a while. They don't want to be associated with anything African. They consider themselves superior to other blacks who don't come from the islands. And Polly really doesn't have a very active social life in Harlem, where she lives."

"Does Chuck object to her weekend visits at your apartment?"

"No, she doesn't get in our way. He doesn't like the sound of the drums on her records when he's trying to study. But Polly can work without accompaniment if I ask her to. She's a very easy person to get along with — as long as you let her dance!"

"Don't you ever do things with her? After all, she's with you almost two days every week."

"Oh, yes," Barbara responded. "Sometimes she asks me to watch her dancing and to tell her what I think. And sometimes we have lunch together when Chuck is on the golf course. She's very bright. Sometimes we talk about conditions in the South, and the way in which blacks are still treated like second class citizens. Polly feels that they don't have enough self-respect. If they knew and cared more about their own culture, they would be proud and would stand up for their rights."

"Is that what Polly wants to do?" Gail asked. "Does she hope to make blacks more aware of their cultural roots?"

"I don't think she has thought this out yet," Barbara answered. "But she has this strong urge to explore her background and that of her people. She says she just has to dance. It was not a conscious decision.”

“Do you remember that questionnaire you did for Dr. Moreley when we were in his class? Did you ever try it on Polly?”

“No,” Barbara responded. “We don’t have much time, and some of the questions might embarrass her. Chuck was right. It is an invasion of privacy sometimes.”

“I don’t think Dr. Moreley uses it anymore.” Gail reported. She was now taking courses with him at the New School for Social Research. “He has a new term now that he calls ‘self-actualization’. Polly seems to be working toward that goal, even if she is not familiar with what it means.”

“Terms don’t really matter.” Barbara responded. “Polly may not be familiar with new ideas in psychology, but she knows where she is going and what she wants to do. She is certainly not a person who is controlled by her environment!”

“She really sounds like an interesting girl. I’d like to meet her sometime. You talk so much about her.” Gail was trying to repress a certain twinge of jealousy. She had seen much less of Barbara since she had begun her association with Polly.

Barbara continued to talk about her new friend whenever she and Gail were together. She described her looks, the strong muscles of her legs, her dark, smooth skin, the intensity of her expression when she was working on her dances.

One time when Gail and Barbara were alone together having lunch, Gail said, “You know, Barbara, you have not stopped talking about Polly since we got here. You seem so excited about her. Are you in love with her?”

Barbara blushed and lowered her eyes. “Maybe I am. I think about her all the time. I’d like to touch her when I watch her dance. Of course, I haven’t done that. We’ve gotten to know a good deal about each other, but our mutual interest in dance is what holds us together. Polly is so single-minded, I don't think she'd have time for anything else."

"Are you more interested in her than you are in Chuck?" Gail asked boldly.

"Of course not!" Barbara responded quickly. "Chuck likes Polly, too. She is so different from other people that we know."

"Is she sensuous?" Gail asked. "You know, I still haven't met her."

"You will. And she will be famous someday. Some of her dances are sensuous. There's lots of hip shaking and undulating movements of the pelvis. But that's part of the African culture. She's not that way when she is not dancing. There's nothing of the flirt or siren about her."

"I bet you wish there were," Gail looked piercingly into her friend's eyes. "You get so excited when you talk about her. You know, Barbara, you ought to see a psychiatrist about your feelings. They could get even more intense and it might affect your marriage."

Gail pursued this idea. She had spoke to Dr. Moreley and he had given her the names of people in the profession that might be helpful. The next time the friends met, they continued the discussion.

"What do I need a psychiatrist for? I'm not sick or anything." Barbara protested.

"Some of these people he recommended are therapists, one or two specializing in sexual adjustments. It wouldn't do you any harm, and it would make me feel better," Gail persisted.

"What has it got to do with you?" Barbara asked.

"Well," Gail hesitated. "It's not easy for me to talk about. We have been such good friends for so long. But I never know how to handle your moments of affection with me. I don't want to encourage you too much, but I don't want to hurt your feelings either."

Barbara blushed and turned her head away. "I didn't know that I was embarrassing you. I like being affectionate with friends. Even as a kid I always had someone close to me. Often I admired an older girl, like a counselor at camp, and tried to establish a relationship with her."

"It was always a girl or a woman, wasn't it? And now it's Polly." Gail looked concerned and she went on. "You know, there are now sex therapists who try to help people with different sexual orientations. Here, take this list and make some phone calls. You can mention that Dr. Moreley recommended them. They all respect him since he has published his books on group dynamics. Most of the people in the field feel that homosexuality can be cured with treatment."

"I don't need to be 'cured'. I like women but I like men too. I have a perfectly good marriage," Barbara was defensive.

"Please try it, for my sake." Gail pleaded "It won't do you any harm, and it may make your marriage better. I don't see the affection with Chuck that you so readily show to me. If it's the money you are worried about, I'd be glad to pay for half of it."

"That's very sweet, Gail. You ARE a good friend. I'll try to talk to one of these people. So much depends on how you get along with a doctor or therapist. It was great talking to Dr. Moreley when we were in his class. His office door was always open so we could come by and talk if we wanted to."

"Well, he's just as open and interested in people as he always was," Gail replied. "But now he's an important man in his field. He's considered one of the founders of the humanist psychology movement. He doesn't do clinical practice. But I'm sure that anyone he recommends will have something of his orientation." Gail was very persuasive and so Barbara agreed to give it a try.

Barbara decided that she would go to see Dr. Michael Rollins, a well-known psychiatrist with an office on Central Park West in New York. He would probably be expensive, but Barbara had faith in him as she had read one of his books. He was an exponent of an interpersonal approach to psychiatry.

Barbara made an appointment several weeks after her phone call since Dr. Rollins' calender was full until then. She thought about her upcoming visit with apprehension. What would the doctor want to know? He was such a busy man. Barbara wondered if her situation was important enough to take up his time. She did not tell Chuck about her appointment, and several times, she thought of cancelling it. But Gail kept telling her how necessary it was for her to see someone. She felt that Dr. Rollins was a fine person to talk to.

When Barbara entered the doctor's office she was greeted warmly by the receptionist. That made her feel better and she relaxed a little as she filled out the initial form. She put down Gail's name in the space that asked who had referred her.

"Oh, you know Gail Stevens? She has been here at one of the seminars Dr. Rollins gives. She seems like such a nice girl, and so interested in her psychology studies."

"She is a good friend of mine," Barbara responded. "She speaks so highly of Dr. Rollins."

"You will like him, too," the receptionist assured her.

Barbara waited only a short time before she was seen. Dr. Rollins was seated behind his desk when she entered the room, but he stood up and came forward to greet her. He escorted her to a comfortable chair near the window.

The curtains were drawn but light came though the sheer fabric, bathing the room in a soft atmosphere. No lamps were lit. There was a chaise off to the side and a large desk with books and papers arranged in small piles on it.

Dr. Rollins took his desk chair and moved it near the window opposite Barbara. "What brings you here, young lady?"

"I really don't know," Barbara spoke quietly, her eyes looking down at her hands in her lap.

"Well, just tell me anything you'd like to say. Relax and make yourself comfortable."

Barbara tried to do as he suggested. "My friend wanted me to come to see you. She thinks I like women too much. You know her. She's studying to be a psychologist and has attended some of your seminars. Her name is Gail Stevens and she's very pretty."

"Yes, I think I remember her. Why does she think you care too much about women?"

Barbara was beginning to talk more freely. "Well, there's this girl I met in a modern dance class. She's very exciting — a black woman with new ideas about doing African dance. I love to watch her and talk to her. She comes to my apartment on weekends to practice her dancing."

"Are you married, Barbara? Do you mind if I call you by your first name?"

"No, I don't mind. And yes, I am married." Barbara smiled for the first time.

"Tell me about your husband."

"He's a great guy," Barbara spoke warmly. "We've known each other a long time. We were in college together. There are things we don't agree about but we usually respect each other's opinions."

"What things do you differ about?"

"Politics mostly. He worries because I've been in what

has been called 'Communist front' organizations. But I'm not a Communist!" Barbara said emphatically. Somehow she felt free talking about this to Dr. Rollins, while she did not discuss it openly to other strangers.

Dr. Rollins nodded, "I understand. It's hard to avoid concern about that today. Tell me more about your relationship with your husband. Are you satisfied with your sexual life?"

"Yes," Barbara answered hesitantly. "I don't get too excited about sex. Before I started going with Chuck, I wasn't really interested in dating, like most girls were. Chuck and I were friends for a long time before we started making love."

"Are you aroused during the lovemaking?" Dr. Rollins voice was calm and he spoke casually.

"I always enjoy it, especially the hugs and the back rubs. I try to respond to Chuck when we have intercourse, but I don't often feel very much."

Dr. Rollins nodded. "Barbara, I'd like to see you one more time. I don't think you will need any extended treatment. You seem like a very healthy and normal girl. However, I want you to understand your own feelings a little more than you do. Come to see me again in about two weeks. In the meantime, I want you to keep track of your fantasies and your reactions to lovemaking with your husband. If you have any emotional experiences with your dancer friend, I'd like to hear about them. Write these things down — just brief notes to remind you of things to tell me when you come here again. Is that all right with you?"

"Yes, Dr. Rollins. Thanks so much for seeing me. I feel better already." Barbara got up and gave her hand to Dr. Rollins, who squeezed it gently and smiled at her.

Barbara followed the doctor's suggestion and made a list of the fantasy thoughts and the emotional and sexual responses she felt in the next two weeks. She was amazed to discover how many fantasies she had. They were brief, and often before she dozed off to sleep. Sometimes they came as daydreams as she was doing some routine thing such as washing dishes. She and Chuck had intercourse three times in the two week period. She felt a light orgasm one time and simply a relaxed feeling of comfort following the other two occasions.

Her fantasies often involved Gail or Polly. She, Barbara, was comforting them when they were under stress. Sometimes her dreams were more bizarre — as when she rescued an unidentified woman from a harrowing experience.

When Barbara returned to Dr. Rollins' office, she recounted these incidents in as much detail as possible. Of course, she could not remember everything. Dr. Rollins helped her. "Do you remember how you felt after these dreams and fantasies?"

Barbara thought a minute. "Well, sometimes I felt excited and happy. That's when I was successful in helping one of the women. Sometimes I woke up before the situation was resolved. Then I felt anxious and jumpy."

"Were any of these dreams about men?"

"I guess not." Barbara responded. "Chuck was there sometimes. Usually he was helping me in some way. In one dream I remember he brought the ladder so I could climb up on the roof to get a cat — but the cat's face was Polly's!"

"What about your daydreams — your fantasies while you are awake?" Dr. Rollins continued in his soft voice.

"They were soothing. Usually I am tired when I have these daydreams — and so is my friend. We have just finished something strenuous and we need to rest together It's very pleasant." Barbara smiled dreamily.

After a little more discussion about Barbara's marital

relations, Dr. Rollins went to his desk and asked Barbara to take the chair opposite him.

"I am going to speak to you frankly, Barbara," the doctor began. "It seems as if you have some homosexual tendencies. But it is nothing to worry about. Many people, both men and women, experience strong feelings toward someone of the same sex. You and your husband seem to have a good marriage. Perhaps you are not as passionate as some other women, but we all have our individual differences. In psychological terms we say that some people possess a stronger libido than others. But that is no different than other preferences. Some people get excited about a football game — others don't. Music is very emotionally involving for some. And then there are placid people who don't get excited about anything. Fortunately, you are not one of these!"

"No." Barbara admitted. "I am usually very enthusiastic about things I care about. Sometimes ideas give me a high. And I can get depressed easily too. I guess I am a moody person."

"Well, it's good to be aware of your own personal qualities. If you care about women, accept it. There's nothing wrong with that, unless you impose yourself on others and expect more in return than they can give comfortably."

"I don't do that, Dr. Rollins. I am very careful not to expect too much of the friends that I love."

"You say that you and your husband enjoy your times together. If there are limitations in what he has to offer you ... that is, if you don't get emotional support for some of the things you care about, as you have told me ... remember that you may have limitations too. Perhaps he would like more passionate responses to his lovemaking."

Barbara looked embarrassed. "I try to be cooperative."

"I am not suggesting that you are inadequate, Barbara.

We all have some limitations. In any marriage that lasts, the partners learn to accept these things."

"Do you think that Chuck will ever understand the way I feel about having my own dancing school?"

"Maybe he will and maybe he won't. Perhaps this is not the right time. You and your husband will have to work these things out."

"We do want to have a family," Barbara confessed. "Maybe I have to put off some of my dreams for a later time."

"Enjoy your marriage, Barbara. You are fortunate to have loving relationships with many people, both male and female."

Dr. Rollins stood up and held out his hand. "Come see me again, Barbara, anytime you feel the need to." Barbara smiled and thanked the doctor. She could not express the gratitude she felt for her improved attitudes after only two sessions. Above all, Barbara carried away with her a sense of relief. Whatever her sexual orientation, she was not abnormal.

COMMENTS

In the fifties, homosexuality emerged more visibly in American society. The war years had opened up the opportunities for gay men and women to be with each other. The groundwork for greater sexual freedom had been laid earlier. The rigid sexual mores of the Victorian period began to disintegrate during the twenties. Thus, in the thirties and forties there was greater acceptance of different patterns of sexual relationships. Kinsey's report on male sexual habits in 1948 and a similar study of the American female in 1953 shattered forever the myth that American adults followed a strict Puritanical code. Among other findings was the fact that a large percentage of the population had sexual experience with someone of the same sex, while even a larger percentage reported sexual inclinations toward same sex individuals.

But in spite of this growing trend in adult behavior, the 1950s witnessed greater restrictions on nonconformity of any kind. As homosexuals emerged more visibly, they became part of the focus of Cold War anxiety. It was thought, in some circles, that homosexuality was spreading like a canker and had to be stopped.

The 1950s witnessed a revitalization of family life. After World War II, the nations experienced a gigantic "baby boom". There was a substantial move to the suburbs and young couples became interested in domesticity. Men worked at gardening and do-it-yourself activities and women took pride in decorating their homes and becoming involved in community activities such as PTA. Individual rebelliousness was frowned upon, and conformity was the tenor of the times.

In a way, the focus upon conformity in family life paralleled the political scene. The Truman Doctrine and the Marshall Plan were attempts to stop the spread of

Communism in Eastern Europe. Joseph McCarthy emerged with his efforts to cleanse the American scene of subversive forces. With the growing hysteria about Communism, homosexuality was similarly under attack. As a matter of fact, in 1954 a congressional committee accused Kinsey of aiding the cause of World Communism. McCarthy preached that Communists corrupted the minds and that homosexuals corrupted the bodies of "good Americans".

It is no wonder that young people, starting out in new careers, feared for their security. In our story, Chuck worried about Barbara's past association with the leftist organizations and insisted that she discard books that might reveal her interest in Marxism. Gail's husband, Arnie, felt that it was the duty of thinking young people to openly oppose the restrictions upon liberty and free speech that were occurring at this time. A kind of schizophrenia was developing in which ardent leftist groups and gay and lesbian groups became more vocal, while at the same time the vast majority of the population became fearful of any association with them. A U.S. Senate Committee on Expenditures in Executive Departments Report asserted:

> *Those who engage in overt acts of perversion lack the emotional stability of normal persons. Indulgence in acts of sex perversion weakens the moral fiber of the individual.* (As quoted in Blumenfeld, Warren and Diana Raymond, 1988).

It is little wonder, then, that psychiatrists and those in related psychological services capitalized on these fears and encouraged homosexuals to try to change their sexual preferences. The notion was popularized that any woman unhappy with a full-time occupation as housewife must be neurotic.

In our story, Gail's insistence that Barbara seek psychiatric help was a reflection of the atmosphere that prevailed in the fifties. Psychiatrists and others in psychological services were promoting the idea that, with intense psychoanalysis, sexual preference could be changed. One practitioner claimed success when a lesbian woman came to him with complaints about insomnia. He encouraged her to sleep with men, which she did. She still had insomnia, but the treatment was considered effective, although the original problem persisted.

Another case, reported by a 1961 Vassar graduate states:

I spent six years going to a psychiatrist trying to learn not be gay. You know what one said? "It's attributable to some aberration in your psychological development." (McKay, 1991)

Interestingly, Freud himself did not see homosexuality as degenerate. Although he considered heterosexuality as "normal", he was aware of the presence of homosexuality in all cultures. He was convinced that there existed a "very considerable measure of latent or unconscious homosexuality ... in all normal people." (Freud, 1963, p. 158, as quoted in Blumenfeld, Warren and Diana Raymond, 1988)

Many of Freud's colleagues treated the development of homosexuality as "unnatural". Most of the post-Freudian theoretical work, right up until 1973 when the American Psychiatric Association removed homosexuality from their list of psychological disorders, discussed homosexuality as a psychological disease. Irving Bieber, for example, terms homosexuality a "hidden but incapacitating fear of the opposite sex", a way to get love and acceptance that had not been provided by their same-sex parent. (ibid. p. 137)

Others claim that women are basically bisexual. Although attracted to men, this attraction develops in addition to the primary homosexual attraction rather than a replacement. Women may have a stronger hold on their gender identity and can allow their sexuality to express itself either in emotional and/or sexual bonding with other women. (Nancy Chodorow, as described in Blumenfeld, Warren and Diana Raymond, 1988)

Doctors are affected by the culture in which they live, just like everyone else. Psychological theories vary at different times in history. It is possible that psychoanalytical attitudes toward homosexuality reflect the old concepts of "good" and "evil". The bible includes passages in which nonreproductive sex is considered to be a sin. The acceptance of psychoanalytical ideas opened up discourse about sexuality, but also provided labels like "perversity" and "deviance" which were used to condemn homosexual activity. (Harvey, Brett, 1993, p. 176)

Even during the fifties, there was a diversity of opinion among psychiatrists and psychologists. As mentioned in our story, a new breed of psychologists became exponents of Gestalt and a more humanist approach to the interpretation of behavior. Other psychoanalysts followed the tenor of the times, condemning homosexuality and attempting to cure it. No doubt they were influenced by the political atmosphere. Some more open-minded psychiatrists and psychologists were more accepting of deviant behaviors and attitudes. Fortunately, Barbara visited one of these, a very prominent clinical psychiatrist who espoused the basic beliefs of the newly-formed Humanist Psychology Association. It took only a few visits to rid Barbara of any sense of guilt and to give her an acceptance of herself and her own sexual inclinations.

Homosexuality and heterosexuality are not mutually exclusive categories. Homosexuals are, of course, a minority group. Bisexuality is probably more common, but women in this category are likely to be discrete about their same-sex relationships. Masters and Johnson have reported that almost all of the individuals they have studied — homosexuals and heterosexuals alike — experienced fantasies involving members of the same sex.

Investigations into the causes of homosexuality have revealed no definitive answers. If we accept differences in human behavior, then the causes of homosexuality are relatively unimportant. Just as being black or left-handed is in no way problematical except in terms of society's treatment, so homosexuality can become an aspect of human behavior which can be accepted without undue guilt or rejection.

REFERENCES

Blumenfeld, Warren J., and Raymond D. *Looking at Gay and Lesbian Life.* Boston: Beacon Press, 23 Beacon St. 02108 (United Universalist Assn. of Congregations), 1988.

Freud, Sigmund. *Civilization and its Discontents.* London: Hogarth Press 1975.

Harvey, Brett. *The Fifties: A Woman's Oral History.* New Harper-Collins, 1993.

Kinsey, A.C. Pomeroy, W.B., and Martin, C.E. *Sexual Behavior in Human Life.* Philadelphia: Saunders, 1948.

Kinsey, A.C., Pomeroy, W.B., Martin, C.E., and Gebhard, P.H. *Behavior in the Human Female.* Philadelphia: Saunders, 1953.

Masters, W.H., Johnson, V.E., and Kolodny, R.C. *Ethical Issues in Sex Therapy and Research.* Boston: Little Brown, 1977.

Matthews, Charles, ed. *Oscars, From A to Z.* New York: Bantam, Doubleday, Dill, 1995.

McKay, Anne. *Wolf Girls at Vassar.* New York: St. Martin's Press, 1992.

FOUR

The 1960s

Marlene's Model

Marlene Appelton gave a good deal of thought to her upcoming photography exhibit. She had never been seen in an art gallery before. Yes, she was well-known in her field. Her pictures had appeared in "Mademoiselle" and "Vanity Fair". She had worked for prestige advertising firms. But she had never had the opportunity to be reviewed by art critics. A New York gallery was offering her this opportunity to be shown, along with two or three other well-known photographers. She needed to appraise her work with a new perspective. She needed to meet different standards.

Marlene looked over her collection of photographs with a discerning eye. There were many fashion poses. There were some abstracts using grill work and collage material. There were landscapes taken on some of her vacation travels. What seemed to be missing were character portraits.

Marlene was thinking about this as she did her shopping at the nearby supermarket. As she strolled down the cereal aisle, she saw her neighbor, Jessica Simon, examining the boxes on the shelf.

"Hi, Jessica," Marlene greeted her. "Are you having difficulty deciding which kind your boys want?"

Jessica looked pensive. "No, that's not what I'm thinking about. The boys make it very clear that they want frosted cereal with football players on the box cover." Jessica's boys were eight and ten years old and very into sports. "How are you doing, Marlene? I don't see you around much lately."

"I'm very busy with my photography work. What about you? How are Michael and the boys?"

Jessica's pensive look returned. "Michael isn't living with us anymore. The boys really miss him."

"What happened?" Marlene looked astonished. "You seemed to be such a perfect family!"

"It's a long story, Marlene. I'm looking for a job now to help tide us over until things get settled. Michael never wanted me to work, and I never finished college, so I'm not prepared to do very much. You are lucky you have your own career and you can still be at home."

Looking at Jessica's expressive face and large, dark eyes, Marlene had an idea. How would it be to ask Jessica to pose for her? She could pay her as a model, even though she had no training.

"Let's stop for a cup of coffee," Marlene suggested. "I have something I'd like to talk over with you."

"Have you tried to get a job yet?" Marlene asked as they sipped their coffee at the corner drug store.

"Yes, but I haven't found anything. The pay is so low, especially for people like me with no training or experience."

"You know," Marlene said, "The colleges now have special continuing studies programs for women like you who want to enter the job market but have only been housewives."

"I've thought about that, but I don't have the money. Besides, most of them have classes that meet at night and I don't have anyone to stay with the boys."

"That really puts you in a bind, doesn't it?" Marlene's voice revealed her feeling of sympathy. "I've been reading about a presidential committee on the status of women that Kennedy has just appointed which will be chaired by Eleanor Roosevelt. You can bet that they'll come up with some plans to help women establish themselves in the economy. Membership on the committee includes people from labor unions and from women's organizations."

"It's about time women got together to promote their own interests." Jessica's face brightened and she suddenly looked animated and involved. "I have read about NOW, that new National Organization for Women. I tried to talk to Michael about it but I think it annoyed him that I was so interested."

Marlene was watching Jessica's face carefully. She was impressed with the rapid changes of expression she exhibited. Her pensive look when they first met was followed by animation and lively interest. Marlene finally decided to broach the topic that had been on her mind when she first asked Jessica to join her for some talk.

"Jessica, would you be interested in posing for me as a model? I need some portrait pictures for a show I've been asked to do. I could pay you by the hour and you could do it while the boys were in school."

Jessica blushed. "That sounds wonderful! But I don't know anything about modeling."

"I can explain what I want," Marlene said. "Let's try it for a while."

They worked together several times and Jessica was a good model. She could be slinky and sexy — her long legs bent with hips tipped forward. She could look like a little girl, wide-eyed and curious, or pouty and sullen. She could be warm and passionate or cold and austere. And all of these moods showed not only in her face but in her body, her hands, the angle of her head. Marlene had only to suggest a time and a person and Jessica fell into the character. She was so real that you would think that the person she was portraying was her whole self.

As the time for the gallery show drew near, Marlene became jittery. Would the art critics come? Would they be kind to her? Her nervousness carried over to her work in the studio. She found herself snapping, "Sit still! This is not one of those action shot windblown things where I go 'click, click, click.' This is a portrait. A woman has lost her child — in an accident or something like that. You take it from there."

Jessica's wide, dark eyes deepened and seemed to sink into her sockets. Her full lips drooped slightly at the corners. Her shoulders slouched. Her long neck tilted to one side and forward a bit. She was lovely, vulnerable and unalterably sad.

Marlene caught her from several angles. Then she tried different lighting and went through the whole process all over again. It was more than an hour before they took a break.

"Jess, I'm sorry. You must be exhausted, hanging in there so long. You were marvelous. I really believed you were grieving."

"I was grieving," Jessica replied. "And what's more, my neck aches."

"Go lie down on the divan." Marlene motioned toward the chaise lounge on the other side of the studio. "We won't be shooting any more for a while. Are you free to stay? I'll send out for some pizza."

"Uh-huh," sighed Jessica. "Michael said he would take the boys to the movies after supper." She walked to the divan and stretched herself out in a position of total relaxation.

Marlene went to the phone on the wall near the door. "Can you send up an eight-inch pizza with everything as soon as possible, please?" She gave her address and added, "Come to the side door and up two flights — then knock."

Marlene's studio was converted from an attic, with a raised dormer picture window that looked out over the ocean. The house was in Neponsit, Long Island, near enough to Manhattan but a block away from the beach. It was an old house, but expensive. Since it was remodeled to include the studio, Marlene could save the extra rental for a city location. Models did not mind taking the thirty-minute ride on the Long Island Railroad to come to the house, and Marlene paid their fare and travel time. There was a separate side entrance so models did not have to come through the house.

Marlene turned away from the telephone and crossed the room to the window. She lifted the blackout shades and gazed out over the rooftops of her neighbors to the ocean. The sky was deep purple with streaks of pink. It was late September, and at seven o'clock daylight was fast disappearing. The view from the window always helped Marlene to relax.

"How fortunate it is to have the studio in my home," Marlene thought. Her husband, Tom, had been so wonderful. He had insisted upon buying this expensive house because he saw the possibilities for setting up the studio for Marlene.

Marlene had known Tom since high school. She had become interested in photography when she began taking pictures of flowers as she and Tom went on nature walks together. They used to go to Palisades Park in New Jersey. They would walk in the woods and Tom would collect "specimens" that he would put under the small microscope, Tom's prized possession. Marlene began photographing leaves and flowers as a means of identifying them. Marlene recalled how Tom helped her to set up a dark room in the basement of her home.

Now Tom was a research chemist and she a professional photographer. "What would have happened if I had not had Tom's support?" Marlene wondered, as she watched the sunlight disappear from the sky. Might she not have problems like Jessica, with no career opportunities and no money for getting training? With Jessica living so nearby, perhaps she could use her for some commercial work coming up soon. Marlene turned away from the window and toward her model.

Jessica was laying on her back, one arm over her head, her eyes half-closed. Marlene walked over and sat on the edge of the divan. "The pizza will be here soon. Turn over and I'll rub your neck."

Jessica obeyed with a small moan, and Marlene began with slow, firm strokes. "How could he leave her?" Marlene thought. She was so lovely — and delicate. Or so it seemed. Marlene knew that Jessica could be strong, positive and very much in control. Everyone thought that Michael adored her, until it was discovered that he was seeing another woman.

Marlene began thinking about her show. She would have an entire alcove of the gallery to herself. She would place some of the landscapes on the left, the abstracts on the right and leave the center for the portraits. "How would it be if I put the mood pictures we have been doing on the center wall, some in large frames and some in small? This one that we did today might be placed in the center if it turns out as well as I expect." Marlene's voice was low, as if she were talking to herself. Her hand continued to move over Jessica's neck, her shoulders and the top of her back.

Marlene became aware of Jessica's even, soft breathing.

She glanced up to find Jessica asleep. "We'll talk about it later," she whispered.

Marlene got up and moved a small table up close to the divan. Then she went to her refrigerator, took out some ice and made iced tea in a small pitcher. Soon there was the sound of steps on the stairs and a knock on the door. The pizza had arrived. Marlene took it, paid the boy and placed the pizza on the table near the divan.

When everything was ready, she touched Jessica lightly on the shoulder. Jessica moved slightly and sighed, her eyes still closed. Marlene stroked her forehead, pushing back a strand of hair that had fallen over her model's eyes.

"I'm awake," Jessica mumbled, stretching and turning onto her back as she did so. "I must have dozed off for a while. I'm sorry."

"Don't be. You needed the rest. Sit up and have your pizza before it gets cold."

Both women sat at the edge of the divan, shoulders close to each other, as they began to eat the pizza and drink the iced tea.

"Umm! Good," said Jessica, a string of melted cheese escaping from the corner of her mouth. Her tongue reached out to retrieve it and she laughed. "This is fun. I feel like a little girl again."

Marlene smiled as she glanced sideways at Jessica. "You are a little girl sometimes. Tell me. How do you change your character so easily? Have you had any acting training?"

"No, never. But I read a lot and I love going to the movies. I guess I have a good imagination, and I can sense how other people might feel."

"You really do a good job of it. Is it emotionally draining for you to do a mood study like today?"

"Yes," Jessica murmured. They had finished the pizza and had turned toward each other. Marlene reached out and took Jessica's hand. The cool, long fingers seemed to unfold as she touched them. Marlene stroked them gently. "Do you miss him, Jess?"

Jessica smiled slowly and her eyes met Marlene's with a brief mischievous look. "The kitchen faucet is still leaking," she said. Marlene laughed. Obviously her friend was not giving away any secrets. Jessica was proud and would never admit to being hurt or feeling rejected. "I'll have to ask Mike, when he comes to get the boys next time, if he could fix it. I hate to pay a plumber for such a little repair, and I'm not good at that sort of thing at all."

They were silent for a while and then Marlene said, "I wonder if Joann is home yet. She went on a picnic with Joe, just the two of them."

"Oh, Marlene, you sound just like an old-fashioned mother! Joe is the young man you don't like so much, is that right?"

"Yes, how did you know?"

"You mentioned him last time I was here, so I could tell."

"Well, he is so much older than she. He has a job already and Joann is still in high school. She seems too young to be going out with him."

"Joann is wiser than you think. She can take care of herself."

Jessica knew Joann since she had recently begun to stay with her boys on a few occasions when Jessica's mother was not available.

"How do you know that?" Marlene asked.

"She has talked to my boys about Mike. They told me. She makes a lot of sense. She seems to understand Mike's nature."

"She does? That's more than I can say for myself!" Marlene raised her eyebrows and shook her head slowly. "I'll never understand how he could leave you. You were such a devoted couple and you had such fun together."

"There are other things." Jess lowered her eyes. "You know about the business. I didn't want Mike to go in with that new partner. I didn't trust him."

"And that's why he left you?" Marlene was astonished.

"I think that's what started it. He needed reassurance from someone else and he found it. The business venture didn't work out well and that made things worse. He couldn't admit I was right."

"You are amazing, Jess. How can you be so understanding and accepting?"

Jessica lowered her eyes and the sad expression she had when she was posing returned. "What can I do about it?" she sighed. Marlene reached out and put an arm around her friend's shoulder. Jessica leaned toward her and her cheek brushed against Marlene's for a brief minute. Marlene's lips touched Jessica's forehead.

A knock on the door startled them. Marlene pulled back and withdrew her hand which had still be holding Jessica's. "Come in," she called.

Tom stuck his head in the doorway, "I thought you might be finished by now. I saw the pizza man come a while ago. Have you had a good session?"

"Yes, very good." said Marlene. They had gone far enough. It was a good time to stop.

COMMENTS:

In the sixties, there were signs of change on many levels involving women. Resistance to the actions of the House of Unamerican Activities Committee rallied women to a common cause. In December of 1962 hundreds of women appeared at the HUAC hearings to protest the investigation of the Women Strike for Peace (WSP) as an organization infiltrated with Communists. Middle-class housewives helped to defeat the HUAC. A new wave of feminine activism emerged which later manifested itself in protests against the Vietnam war and the emergence of organizations such as National Organization for Women (NOW) and other women's groups.

The media was quick to pick up on this new trend, suddenly discovering the "trapped housewife". "Twice as many women attended college as before, leading *Newsweek* to worry about 'Young Wives with Brains: Babies, Yes — But What Else?'" (*Newsweek*, 55, March 9, 1960: 57-60)

The majority of women remained housewives, but there was a continuing conflict between the restrictive cultural definition of a woman's domestic role and women's growing interest in participating in more creative, community-related activities. (Lopata, 1971)

By the mid-sixties, the economy of the fifties was in decline and there were fewer opportunities for men in the job market. Divorce rates were rising and the need for middle-class women to seek employment was increasing.

Although neither of the women in our story was involved in the women's movement directly, they were, nevertheless, affected by it. Jessica was struggling with maintaining her lifestyle, after her change in marital status. She was aware of her need for further education, but felt she could not afford to pursue it. A few universities had begun experiments to help women cope with their "dual role" as housewives and their need to work outside the home in some capacity. The continuing education movement opened higher education to women who had been "housewives" but who wanted to enter the labor force in meaningful jobs. (Evans, 1989, p. 265)

Marlene was also aware of the changes in the status of women, and was grateful that she could combine homemaker with career so successfully. Both women were interested and enthusiastic about political developments that might improve the status of women in society.

Marlene and Jessica established a working relationship that was beneficial to both. The women's movement, in which they did not play an active part, nevertheless, enabled them to achieve self respect and affirmed their need for the growing relationship between them.

After a while their working relationship leads to empathy and physical attraction. The extent of this relationship cannot be determined. The attraction may only exist when the women are working together, or it may persist in fantasy for either one of them. Marlene appears to have a good marriage and her friendship with Jessica probably does not affect this. Jessica, recently divorced, may welcome Marlene's affection. She is a sensual person to whom physical responses come naturally.

Friendships of this nature were commonplace in the nineteenth and the beginning of the twentieth centuries. Lillian Faderman (1981, 1991) has chronicled many of these woman-loving-woman relationships which she calls "romantic friendships". She quotes the psychologist, Charlotte Wolff, as observing: "It is not homosexuality but homoaffectionality which is the center and the very essence of women's love for each other ... the sex act is always secondary with them."

While practicing homosexuals are a minority group, the

interest in homosexuality is widespread. Dr. John Money of Johns Hopkins, (quoted by Phil Donahue, 1985) says: "Everyone has a homosexual side ... we can be attracted to both sexes." Dr. Money attributes this element of bisexuality in all of us to the fundamental bisexuality of the human fetus. For the first few weeks after conception, the fetus is both male and female, and it continues to carry the legacy of that bisexuality even after it begins to differentiate according to its chromosomal sex. "No matter what we become," says Dr. Money, "male or female, we always carry some hint of our early bisexual nature." Zoologists have observed homosexual play in most higher mammals. If this is a common phenomenon in animals, it is not surprising to find manifestations of this instinct in human beings.

It is to be noted that Marlene is quick to hide any evidence of affection for Jessica when her husband appears at the door. Although Tom seems to be accepting of Marlene's career which is independent of his life with her, Marlene fears resentment if Tom were to become aware of her feelings for Jessica. Even when men are accepting of their wife's independence, they do not like to see them becoming too intimate with their women friends. In the sixties, lesbian relationships were often covert and some women maintained satisfactory marriages while still having a love relationship with a friend. This may be the case with Marlene and Jessica.

REFERENCES

Donahue, Phil. *The Human Animal.* New York: Simon and Shuster. 1985.

Evans, Sara M. *Born for Liberty.* New York: The Free Press/MacMillan, 1989.

Faderman, Lillian. *Odd Girls and Twilight Lovers.* New York: Columbia University Press, 1991.

Faderman, Lillian. *Surpassing the Love of Men.* New York: William Morrow and Co., 1981.

Gallese, Liz Roman. *Women Like Us.* New York: William Morrow and Co., 1985.

Lopata, Helena Z. *Occupation: Housewife.* New York: Oxford University Pres, 1981.

Money, J. and A. Ehrhardt. *Man and Woman, Boy and Girl.* Baltimore, Md.: Johns Hopkins University Press, 1972.

Newsweek 55, March 7, 1960: 57-60

Singer, June. *Androgyny.* Garden City: Anchor Press/Doubleday, 1976.

FIVE

The 1970s

Career Moms

Tracy and Jennifer met at a Lamaze class for expectant mothers. They knew each other slightly since they had attended the same graduate business program. Both women were working and it was difficult to get to class on time. Frequently they came right from work, without taking time for dinner. After class they would go out for a bite to eat, and a chance to talk.

The first session was introductory. Since many of the women were working, a discussion was led about maternity leave: "How much time are you allowed?" "How much time will you need?" "Is your leave paid or unpaid?" The answers to these questions varied considerably. Different companies had different policies. At dinner that evening the two women discussed those questions.

"I think I will be able to take a leave, but I don't know for how long." Tracy worked for a new personal computer company. She was the first member of the staff to become pregnant. "I know others have gotten 'disability leave' but I never heard of 'maternity leave'. I am certainly going to find out about it right away."

"My firm is a large chain of high fashioned clothing stores," Jennifer said. "I guess they have some overall policy, but I have not heard about it. I may have to take time off on my own."

"Well," Tracy said, "It's about time these big companies took these things into consideration. I bet a firm like yours hires mostly women. They should have a specific amount of time allowed for them to have babies."

Jennifer looked concerned. "I'm glad our instructor brought that up tonight. Most of us would wait for the last minute to investigate, and that's too late. After all, we have to make financial adjustments, or hire a baby nurse or something if our jobs are in jeopardy. I have been reading about maternity leave. It was discussed at that conference commemorating the 50th anniversary of women's suffrage. I believe they passed a bill recommending it."

Tracy reacted with fervor. "My father's union made recommendations like that and they have written to congressmen. He works in the garment industry and many of the employees are women. So far, I think they just take a leave of absence without pay, and they are lucky if their jobs are waiting for them when they come back."

Jennifer retorted, "That's not fair! I know that some countries in Europe provide maternity leave. It's about time that our government took some action to protect the rights of pregnant women."

Tracy picked up this idea right away. "Well, we may be the first in our companies to request maternity leave. Maybe we can negotiate a deal which might benefit women in the future."

The two women planned to keep in touch with each other

after the Lamaze course was over. They would make a concerted effort to tell other women about the need for maternity leave.

"You just have to plan carefully," said Tracy. "You are taking a risk if you take too much time out. How can you be sure your job will be waiting for you?" Tracy spoke in very positive fashion as she looked directly at Jennifer.

"I really don't know as yet how much time I will need," Jennifer was less certain. "I will have to see how things work out."

Husbands were supposed to come to the next session, as it was required in Lamaze method that a "coach" be available at all times, for the training program as well as for the delivery. The two women planned to ask their husbands to join them for dinner the next week.

Tracy's husband, Keith Adams, was handsome, with a gentle quality and sweet smile. He looked at Tracy adoringly as she talked. He was an executive in the same firm in which Tracy worked. They had married shortly after Tracy had graduated from a state college in Rhode Island and had come to Boston to take her first job with Keith's company. Tracy had been flattered that an executive in the company would be interested in her! She came from a working-class family and had gone through college on scholarships and work-study jobs. She was the first member of her family to attend college, and she was anxious to rise above her humble background.

Jennifer had attended Brandeis, a prestige college near Boston. She married a young doctor, David Ellis, who had just graduated from Harvard Medical School. He had been invited to become part of a research team in cardiology at Massachusetts General Hospital where he had done his residency. Jennifer had worked for a few years before going back to college to get a Masters in business administration.

The Ellis' were definitely an upward mobile couple.

The men got along well with each other from their first meeting. They both took pride in the wives' accomplishments. At the dinner table, Keith asked David, "What do you think of this Lamaze program? As a doctor, you should understand more about it."

"I think it's great," David replied. "The exercises help the women to take a more active part in the delivery, and this is good for their mental attitude. Having husbands there to be part of the action is an asset psychologically for both the woman and the man involved."

"I like it well enough," Keith said, "but I think they make too much of a fuss about the atmosphere. I read somewhere that Lamaze himself wants the room darkened when he attends to a birth. The stroking of the infant seems good, but lots of healthy babies came into this world after getting a good slap on the backside at delivery!"

"That may be," David agreed. "I don't know how much the infant experiences at that stage. We do know that a lot of learning takes place almost from birth and even in the womb. Certainly gentle treatment of the infant at delivery won't do any harm, and may be very beneficial."

Keith shook his head slowly. "Not everybody can afford this program, though. And the doctors are not likely to have all the time it takes in the delivery room. I'm not sorry we are doing it. It's an experience I am glad I can share with Tracy."

Fortunately, the two women had relatively easy deliveries. Since it was a first child for both of them, this was rather unusual. Both Tracy and Jennifer thought that the Lamaze breathing exercises had helped. The cooperation of their husbands was a strong factor in making the entire process of pregnancy and giving birth more pleasurable.

The couples remained friendly and continued to see each

other. When they could afford to buy a house, they both moved to Swampscott, within commuting distance from Boston. The nearness to the beach made it ideal for weekend outings with the children which both couples enjoyed. They spent many weekends together while the children enjoyed playing and Jennifer, Tracy and their husbands compared notes about their families, their jobs and their futures. Tracy's son, Jonathan, and Jennifer's daughter, Sarah, were the same age. Since their mothers had been in the Lamaze program together, the children knew each other from infancy. They acted almost like siblings, but there were some differences.

At the age of four, Sarah began to assert her femininity. One day at the beach, when they were building sand castles, Sarah asked Jonathan, "Would you mind going down to the ocean and getting me some water?" Jennifer overheard this request and said, "Sarah, you are a big girl, you can get your own water in your pail."

"I know that, Mommy," Sarah whispered in her mother's ear. "Shh — don't tell him! Boys are supposed to help girls."

Jennifer stared at Sarah in amazement, "Where did you get that idea, Sarah? You know that Daddy and I share all the chores around the house. I don't expect Daddy to do things for me that I can do myself."

Tracy overheard this conversation and chuckled. "You may not teach it, Jen, but somehow Sarah acquired the notion that ladies need to rely on male support. Children assimilate ideas about sex roles even if they do not see them practiced at home!"

Tracy went back to work after five weeks as she had planned, leaving the baby in the hands of a capable housekeeper. Jennifer remained at home and had another child before returning to work.

Neither of the women had given up the pursuit of her career. Tracy was promoted several times. She kept up with the rapidly changing field of computer science and took refresher courses from time to time. She became sales manager for the New England region, which required traveling a good deal. Fortunately she had capable household help. Keith became the "primary parent," taking their son Jonathan to day care and picking him up every day.

Keith seemed to enjoy this role. He was interested in seeing his son develop emotionally and socially. He was supportive of Tracy's career and did not seem to mind that she earned more money than he did. Keith did not have Tracy's all-consuming drive and consequently did not advance his position with the firm as fast as she did.

Jennifer enjoyed being home with Sarah, and it was less than two years before her son, Danny, was born. When he was ready for day care, Jennifer decided to go back to work. She was immediately placed as an assistant buyer for the stores in the Boston area. She was happy doing this, but Jennifer knew that major buying was done out of the New York office. An offer was made to transfer her there at a considerable raise in salary.

She discussed this with David immediately. "Of course, I'd like to be in New York. Our main office there buys for all of the stores, and my job here is simply sending our needs to them. It would be much more exciting to go into the market and make the selections. But what about you? You've done so well in your practice here."

"I think I could do well in New York too. I have connections there. The research project is almost finished, but we have already been published in professional journals. I am sure my name is known in some of the big cardiology offices in New York. Why don't I contact them and see what I can do about relocating?"

"Would you really do that, David? That would be wonderful." She hugged her husband as she said this.

"We might try it," David replied hesitantly. "We could rent our house here and see how things worked out before we made a final move. You have managed so well as a wife and mother, even after you went back to work."

Jennifer sensed the hesitancy in her husband's voice. It would be difficult for David to start up a practice in a different city, even if his name was known in the profession. She experienced a certain amount of guilt for suggesting this.

Shortly after this conversation, David and Jennifer went to see a new picture, "Kramer vs. Kramer". A divorce resulted from the woman's need to find her own identity after years of serving as wife and mother. Her husband was a busy advertising man who spent little time at home and seemed unaware of his wife's growing loss of self esteem.

As they left the movie, Jennifer began the discussion. "Do you think she was right to walk out on her husband and son? I don't know what I would have done if you were not so understanding."

"No," David replied. "She needed some support and companionship, but leaving her family was a desperate move. It was an interesting story and I guess it touched home for many modern couples."

"David, are you sure it's O.K. for me to take that buyer's position in New York? Am I letting you and the children down by making a change at this time?"

David was reassuring. "Look, hon, we always said we would go wherever the opportunities were better for one of us. Well, that time has come, and we should take advantage of it. If it doesn't work out after a year, we can come back to Boston. I think it would be an interesting change for both of us. The kids are young enough that they will readjust quickly to a new environment. New York is an exciting place to live and there will be lots of new experiences for all of us."

"David, you're terrific!" Jennifer exclaimed. "How many husbands would be willing to relocate because of their wives' jobs?"

The Ellis family soon moved to New York. As Jennifer said to Tracy when she told her of the move, "I am so proud of David. He really respects me as an equal partner."

Tracy missed Jennifer after she moved to New York, and so, when she got a call at work from Eileen, a former classmate at graduate school, she welcomed talking to her. They planned to meet for lunch the next day.

Eileen had always been unpredictable. Classmates at school either disliked her or were fascinated by her. She was small, pert and animated. She seemed to take over in any crowd where she appeared.

She bounced into the tea room at the Hyatt Hotel in a flimsy chiffon dress with spaghetti straps. She had said she was in Boston on a business trip but her appearance was far from business-like. Her reddish-blonde hair flew out behind her as she rushed through the door.

"I'm sorry I'm late," she said, as she slid into the seat on the bench opposite Tracy. "You look great! I hear you're doing well in your job. The computer outfit has come up in the world since you joined the firm!" Eileen kept up a stream of lively talk that hardly gave Tracy a chance to get a word in edgewise. She talked about her own career — how they had wanted to make her a partner in the consultant firm where she worked, but she had refused.

"Why did you do that?" Tracy was incredulous. "I thought you were as ambitious as the rest of us at school. I just couldn't wait to get back to work after the baby came."

"I know. I like my job too. I like dealing with clients and making suggestions to them about their businesses. I am usually right too, but I don't want to be married to my firm. I want the freedom to go and do what I like. Big business executives don't have that."

Tracy smiled. "I remember at school you were always running off for weekend cruises and what not! Yet, you always did well on tests and reports in class. I used to envy you. I had to work so hard."

Eileen gave her a pixie-like grin. "It was fun to try to kid around with the professors. They usually liked my comments in class, although some thought I was fresh!"

"You always got away with it though. Did you ever marry again? I remember you had a baby and your mother was taking care of him for you."

"Yes, Rudy, that's short for Rudolfo, he's a wonderful boy. He's ten years old and he lives with me now. He goes to private school and is dropped off at home at four o'clock. Sometimes he gets dinner ready for me! He sees his father in the summertime. He's in Jamaica with him now. I put him on the plane just last week."

"He flies by himself?" Tracy asked.

"Of course. He's very capable and independent. His father will pick him up at the airport. Oh, you should see him! He's very good-looking — like his dad — tall and thin — coffee-au-lait skin, big black eyes — and a grin that lights up his whole face."

Eileen had been married for a short time to a Jamaican whom she had met as a teenager. Her family had taken frequent trips to the Caribbean and Eileen, at sixteen or seventeen had already had several romantic adventures. She still traveled in mixed ethnic groups and was friendly with her ex-husband whom she saw whenever he came to New York. Eileen went on to talk about her friends, her "ex" and the way in which her young son fit into all of these groups.

Tracy was intrigued with her stories. "I remember how everyone was so curious about you. Your lifestyle was so different from the rest of us. You never married again?"

"Hell no! Why should I do that? I'm lucky I have Rudy, and I have lots of friends from all over the world. When they visit me, I have a different life with each one of them. One guy is from Kuwait and he's very rich. His father owns oil wells. When he's in New York, we have a wild time. He has two or three sports cars and we go to the races and meet his Arab friends. They love to bet on the horses and they usually win. When my girlfriend from Hollywood visits, we go to all the shows and she knows the producers and a lot of show people. She just got her first script accepted by one of the big studios, so it looks like she will be in California for awhile. I really miss her. We were very close."

"I miss Jennifer," Tracy confessed. "You remember her. She married the doctor and they had a baby the same time I had Jonathan. She has another child now — a little boy, and they have moved to New York because Jennifer got a big offer from the buying office there. We used to talk to each other almost every day before she left."

"She is in New York now? You'll have to give me her address. She was always a classy dame." Eileen's speech pattern was full of colloquialisms, resembling street talk rather the more formal patterns of the business world. "I'd really like to see her."

For the next few days, Tracy could not get Eileen out of her mind. Her breezy manner, her throaty voice, her animation were fascinating. Tracy even thought about her bare shoulders with the thin spaghetti straps, so unlike the tailored outfits she and her business colleagues wore.

The next time the women met was for dinner. It was Keith's bowling night and Jonathan was home with the housekeeper, so Tracy decided to stay downtown and spend the evening with her new-found friend. After dinner they went back to Eileen's room in the hotel, where she was staying for the week.

"Would you like a drink? Eileen asked. "I have a portable bar I always carry with me." She opened a leather case with small bottles of assorted wines and liquors. "How about a brandy?"

"That would be fine." Tracy sank into a deep armchair and kicked off her shoes. "You don't mind if I get comfortable?"

"No. Matter of fact, I think I'll change into something cozier." Eileen had been wearing a red sports jacket and white slacks with a nautical insignia. After a few minutes in the bathroom she reappeared in shorty pajamas with a lace jacket to match. She stretched out on the bed, propping the pillows up behind her, and reached for her glass of brandy. Her eyes seemed to smile as she looked over the rim of the glass at Tracy. "How is your love life?" she asked boldly.

"Oh, it's O.K."

"You don't sound very enthusiastic. As I remember, Keith was such a good-looking man. You used to be crazy about him."

"Yes." Tracy responded. "He was an executive in the firm where I had just been hired when I met him. But that was years ago. He's still in the same position and I outrank him now. He just doesn't seem to have the drive and ambition you need to get ahead."

Eileen thought for a moment. "You know, Tracy, everyone is not made the same way. You have such terrific drive. No one could keep up with you. Do you mean your sex life has gone stale?"

"In a way. There's just no time. I put in twelve to sixteen hours a day, and often I'm on the road and don't get home for days. Keith is great. He never complains about that and he spends a lot of time with Jonathan. They get along so well together."

"People always find time for things they like the most. Don't you think you are missing a lot? That's why I didn't accept that promotion. I don't want business to be my whole life. There are lots of other things I like to do." Eileen winked mischievously.

"Well," Tracy replied. "To me, work is the most fundamental thing in my life. My work identifies me as the person I am."

"You're too serious, Tracy! Come sit on the bed. I want to show you something."

Tracy moved over toward the end of the bed and Eileen stretched her legs toward her. "See this!" Eileen continued, "I got this scar from a fall when I was skiing. But it is such fun and so exciting, I wouldn't give it up no matter how many falls I take!"

Tracy ran her hand along the scar. "It's quite deep. It must have been a bad fall."

"That feels nice." Eileen leaned against the pillow, her eyes half-closed. Would you mind putting some lotion on my back? I must have gotten a burn out there on the yacht today."

"I thought you said you were working?"

"I was. The yacht belongs to one of my clients. That's why I'm in Boston. I have been working with him all week. Today we decided to finish up on the yacht so we took our papers along and spent the day there." Eileen reached into the night table drawer and brought out some skin lotion. She gave it to Tracy. "Thanks a lot, hon. Come lie here and I'll turn over. It's my shoulders that feel hot."

Tracy found it hard to resist Eileen. No wonder she always got everything she wanted! She was so seductive, yet her manner was playful. She did not seem to be taking anything very seriously.

Soon Tracy's head was on the pillow next to Eileen's.

She turned on her side in order to reach Eileen's far shoulder. Neither of the women talked for a while, and then Tracy felt Eileen's small hand reaching between her legs. She opened her pants zipper and allowed the fondling to continue.

Eileen whispered softly, "See, it doesn't take much time, and if you like it, you can always make room for it."

Tracy felt a warm glow and a tingling sensation she had not felt in years. She kissed Eileen's cheek — and then her lips. "I have never done anything like this before," she murmured.

"It's nice, isn't it?" Eileen responded, pressing closer to Tracy. "I hope this won't be the last time."

It was not the last time. Tracy visited Eileen in her hotel room once more before Eileen had to return to New York. After that, they arranged to meet periodically when Tracy was "on the road" for business. Eileen always managed to get away for a day to meet Tracy in Hartford, New Haven, or elsewhere along Tracy's New England circuit.

The women enjoyed their time together but neither of them thought of it as a serious affair. Eileen continued to have various relationships with her many friends, her clients and her ex-husband. Her zest for life was insatiable and no one could pin her down, or keep up with her.

Eileen taught Tracy to "lighten up". Strangely enough, she began to enjoy her physical relationship with her husband more. Orgasms were more frequent, although never very intense. Somehow Eileen had awakened erotic feelings in Tracy that had laid dormant for years.

Keith noticed the difference. One night as they lay in bed together he commented, "Hon, you seem to be enjoying our times in bed together more. I've been trying to arouse you for years, but now it seems to be working." Keith looked over at Tracy shyly and she smiled.

"Yes, I am enjoying lovemaking more. I guess I am more relaxed than I used to be. I am not as anxious about my job, too. I met an old friend from grad school, Eileen. She is a very successful business consultant, but she doesn't let her work control her whole life. She's been talking to me about not taking my work too seriously nor letting my career dominate everything."

"I remember Eileen," Keith said. "You used to talk about her. She was always running off somewhere to parties or ski trips or someplace. Is she still as wacky as ever?"

"Yes," Tracy replied. "I suppose so, but she has a big executive job, a ten-year-old son and an ex-husband who still visits her. She's in New York but she comes to Boston on business sometimes. I meet her for lunch occasionally. I gave her Jennifer's address and maybe they'll get together in New York. Really, I don't know how Eileen has time for all the things she does."

"I'd like to meet her sometime," Keith responded, "She sounds like an interesting gal."

"Oh, she is that!" Tracy tried to sound casual but she was afraid that her lively interest in Eileen was beginning to show. "However," she added quickly, "Eileen is not here too often, and usually it is during the daytime. I don't think you could get away."

Tracy began to spend more time with Keith and their son and she found the family relationship growing stronger. Keith was a sweet guy and Tracy grew fonder of him as time went by. Being with him was never as exciting as the times she spent with Eileen, but, Tracy thought, "There is room in the life of a modern career woman for many kinds of relationships."

COMMENTS

In the years during and after World War II, millions of women had joined the labor force, many of them leaving home to take jobs. But the expansion of the 'sphere' occurred without fanfare and was not accompanied either by progress toward equality or an organized effort to protest traditional definitions of 'woman's place'" (Chafe, 1991, p. 194)

But in the sixties, the woman's movement changed all that. Women became aware of injustices done to them because of their sex. A series of preconditions made this change possible. Political unrest, protest, and a social atmosphere conducive to reform existed. Young people were protesting the Vietnam War. Racial segregation was being confronted and there were marches in the South along with efforts to get out the Black vote. Women became involved in some of these causes, and along the way, there was a growing awareness of women's rights.

Every movement needs a catalyst to initiate protest. The most widely noted indictment of America's system of sex inequality came from the pen of Betty Friedan. According to her, American women had been held captive by a set of ideas that defined female happiness as total involvement in the role of wife and mother. In her book, "The Feminine Mystique" (1982, 20 Anniversary Ed.), she charged that a woman's horizons were circumscribed from childhood on the assumption that her highest calling in life was to be a servant to her husband and children.

The protest movement that took place in the 1960's and 1970's involved demonstrations at professional meetings to demand equal employment opportunities. There was a national strike to commemorate the 50th anniversary of woman's suffrage. There were numerous articles in newspapers and magazines deploring the "oppression" of women in the work place and in society as a whole.

Women growing up in the sixties began to expect more from life than dishwashing, picking up, ironing and folding diapers. They felt a need to develop an identity of their own. They generally planned to pursue their own careers and to postpone marriage and having babies for a later time. Many decided to place career before the demands of domesticity, and did not contemplate marriage at all.

For career-oriented women in the fifties and sixties, it was usually a matter of choice: career or marriage. Sometimes marriage came first, and then the restrictions imposed by it caused rebellion, and frequently divorce. The movie "Kramer vs. Kramer" (Stanley Jaffe Productions, Columbia, 1979) portrayed a woman's conflict when she felt the need to establish her own identity, in spite of husband and child. The popularity of this movie and the many Academy Awards it won, is testimony to the prevalence of this kind of thinking in the late seventies.

In the sixties women planned to pursue careers and often attended college to prepare for them. By the mid-seventies, these career-oriented women had entered the work force. Some extended their education into graduate programs, attending medical school, law school or master's programs in business administration or computer science. Whereas teaching and nursing seemed to be the only avenues for careers outside the home in the past, the seventies and eighties found women entering law or becoming top-level executives in business.

The stories about Tracy, Jennifer and Eileen deal with career-oriented women who placed career ahead of, or on a par with, family responsibilities. But problems existed in spite of their determination.

The question of relocation affected the marriage of Jennifer and David. They had agreed to locate wherever the position was most desirable, whether the choice favored

David's career or Jennifer's. In the first years of their marriage, David won out, since his placement as a doctor pursuing medical research kept the couple in Boston even though Jennifer preferred New York. Years later, after the birth of two children, they decided to make the move to New York because of Jennifer's job opportunities. Jennifer experienced a certain amount of guilt making this decision, since it was customary to consider the husband to be the major wager-earner and therefore to get primary consideration in deciding upon location for the family.

Unusual as it was, the Ellis family made the move based upon the woman's career — a new step in the struggle for equality for women. The Adams family was also atypical, since Keith took major responsibility for his son, Jonathan, as Tracy's position took her out of town so often. Eileen, also, was able to maintain a good relationship with her son while holding down a responsible executive job and living a multifaceted social life.

Although none of these women were active feminists, their attitudes and expectations were influenced by the feminist activism that was happening all around them in the seventies. Being a "super-mom" was not easy for them and some problems did arise.

Tracy's marriage became unsatisfactory mainly because of her success in business. Working in the same company, she outstripped her husband and advanced to higher executive positions. Keith had become the "primary parent" and was responsible for taking their son, Jonathan, to and from nursery school and attending to their parental duties. This is a role he seemed to enjoy. He adored his wife and was thoroughly supportive of her career. Yet the physical attraction between them seemed to diminish. Although Tracy appreciated all of his help at home, she seemed to lose some respect for him, and no longer enjoyed his physical advances.

Keith wondered what he could do to please her. Tracy ultimately sought satisfaction in her relationship with Eileen.

Another common problem of working mothers occurs when a child is ill. If he or she attends day care or nursery school, that is not possible during illness. Children usually want the company of a parent at times like these. Baby sitters and domestics cannot always cope with these problems.

Harvey (1993, p. 172) reports the feelings of a mother who was to begin as an assistant professor at a nearby college. Her son developed a severe diaper rash in the care of an incompetent babysitter. The mother was about to quit work, but decided to discuss it with her doctor, who sent her to a psychiatrist. He told her that she should apply the same intelligence that she applied to work to getting adequate child care. Being insightful and ahead of his times, the doctor said he thought the mother would do more harm than good by giving up her career and staying home.

This worked out, but the ordeal took its toll on the mother's career. She made the mistake of discussing her problems with colleagues. As a result, she was not promoted to a tenured professorship for which she had been considered. She thought, "If a man goes and talks to his colleagues about prostate cancer or whatever, they are sympathetic and supportive. If a woman says she is having trouble getting good child care, they view this as crippling." (Harvey, 1993, p. 174)

The problems of a working mom become even more complicated when a couple gets divorced. Eileen's son Rudy, had to shift for himself a good deal of the time. He became a "latchkey child", but fortunately he was competent enough to handle it.

The divorce rate soared during the seventies. A pool taken in 1979 showed divorce up 67 percent since 1968 (Chronicle of America, 1992). The report showed that the average marriage lasted 6.6 years. Forty percent of children surveyed came from one parent homes.

The seventies were noted for an increase of books about sex. It was during the seventies that the famous Master and Johnson studies were published. These published works affected family values. Changes in family structure were certain to affect marital relations as well as relations among women.

Career moms had new problems to share with each other. Without the macho male image to respect and depend upon, women had to make decisions on their own. The "super-mom" who could handle career, home and children was a product of the seventies. Although she was doing what she wanted to do, and could not deny that she had achieved a strong self-image, her life was not without stress. Jennifer, Tracy and Eileen each had problems that were unique to their career-oriented lives.

REFERENCES

Chafe, William H. *The Paradox of Change: American Women in the 20th Century.* New York: Oxford University Press, 1991.

Daniel, Clifton, ed. director. *Chronicle of America.* Mt. Kisco, N.Y.: Chronicle Publications, 1992.

Fourth World Conference for Women, Beijin, China, 1995. *Advancing Gender and Equality.* Washington D.C. The World Bank, 1995.

Frieden, Betty. *The Feminine Mystique.* (20th Anniversary Edition) New York: Norton, 1983.

Gallese, Liz Roman. *Women Like Us.* New York: Morrow, 1985.

Harvey, Brett. *The Fifties: A Woman's Oral History.* New York: Harper Collins, 1993.

Konek, Carol Wolfe and Sally L. Kitch. *Women and Careers: Issues and Challenges.* Thousand Oaks, CA: Sage Publications, 1994.

Matthews, Charles. *Oscars From A to Z.* New York: Doubleday, 1995.

Sweet, Robin and Patty Bryan, *The Working Woman's Lamaze Handbook.* New York: Hyperion, 1992.

SIX

The 1980s

A Substitute Lover

Jack was such a capable man — an organizer, an athlete, an artist. There was nothing around the house that he could not fix. He collected odds and ends and always found use for them. He made beautiful silver jewelry. Each piece had its own original design. He wouldn't sell his jewelry. It was for his wife, Sue, and a few close friends to cherish.

When Jack developed Parkinson's disease, his coordination was the first thing to go. How difficult for one so capable to have to ask for help to turn on the TV!

Later Jack developed a heart condition and had frequent angina attacks. He had to have oxygen administered in order to be relieved. Even when having an attack, Jack would say, "I need some oxygen, Sue, but there's no rush if you are busy. Finish what you are doing first."

Of course, Sue responded immediately. Jack's acceptance of his condition and his desire not to impose on anyone was remarkable — but then, he was always like that. He never wanted to "put anyone out". She knew this, and although she was always there when he needed her she didn't fuss over him. She knew about his pride and how uncomfortable it would make him feel to be dependent on anyone all of the time.

Sue tried to explain this to friends but they did not seem to understand. "Are you feeling all right today, Jack?" "Can I get you something?" Of course, friends meant well, but Sue sensed how Jack must feel when he was treated like a child. He was such a proud and independent man. He began to withdraw from conversation — he who had been a raconteur — a leader of groups, a well-loved administrator of a school. He seemed now to be so timid and insecure. It was painful for Sue to see.

Only Maryann seemed to understand. She greeted Jack casually when he came with Sue to social occasions. But after a while, she took every opportunity to "kid around" with him. She sat on his lap, she hugged him, she flirted with him. His old smile returned (he DID like women!) and he seemed like the Jack he used to be.

Maryann had been fond of Jack long before his illness. He had come from a background similar to hers and she identified with his sentiments about his childhood. She and Jack had grown up in the same small city in upstate New York. Although they didn't know each other well at that time, they had many memories of people and places they both were able to recall.

Once Sue had invited Maryann to join her and Jack for a summer vacation at a hotel near Jack's childhood home. He and Maryann enjoyed reminiscing about their childhood experiences.

"Do you remember the stationery store that used to be on that corner?" Maryann asked Jack. "It's a fancy chain drug store now, but I bet they don't make those 2¢ plain drinks we used to have!"

Jack was in a wheelchair most of the time, and Sue and Maryann took turns pushing him. They joked about their handicaps. Sue had a recent hip replacement and Maryann had a chronic osteoporosis condition with frequent broken bones. Since all three of them had to use canes occasionally, they decided to make the most of it. They did a parody to "Doin' What Comes Naturally" from Irving Berlin's musical, "Annie Get Your Gun", and presented it in the dining room at the hotel one evening:

Trio:　　　　Folks with canes can still have fun
　　　　　　　　Of this we are most certain
　　　　　　Lost of things to do and see
　　　　　　　　If you do them naturally!

Jack:　　　　I once played golf and tennis
　　　　　　　　And even won a prize.
　　　　　　Now I watch them on TV
　　　　　　　　'Cause I know that time sure flies!

Sue:　　　　And I was once a dancer
　　　　　　　　Ballet and tap and jazz
　　　　　　I even made up my own steps
　　　　　　　　And was known for my "Kazass!"

Maryann:　　Now I was not a great athlete
　　　　　　　　Music was what I did best
　　　　　　I played piano nicely
　　　　　　　　Now my fingers need a rest!

Trio:　　　　So here we are at Blue Lodge Inn
　　　　　　　　Enjoying every minute
　　　　　　Being the best that we can be
　　　　　　　　Doin' what comes naturally!

Everyone at the hotel enjoyed the trio's performance and they had to repeat it frequently at dinner time or during the evening's entertainment. Jack was livelier at this time than he had been for months. Somehow he and Maryann seemed to have a small romance budding between them. Sue enjoyed their laughter together, although she realized that the gaiety couldn't last. At night, Jack's angina attacks came more frequently and lasted longer. Sue was grateful to Maryann for giving Jack this much fun.

But until Jack died, Maryann had only a casual relationship with Sue. In some ways Sue was only Jack's wife. The three of them had great times together, but the sparks really flew only between Jack and Maryann.

Jack died just a month after their vacation together and Maryann became very attentive to Sue. She stopped by often with "goodies" — a carrot cake she had made, a single flower from her garden, sometimes a package of candy or crackers that were favorites of Sue's. These were not just condolences from a friend. They were indications of concern and affection.

Soon Maryann began to fill the gap left by Jack's absence. She listened as Sue told her of some of the problems they had during their long marriage. Maryann had been divorced, and though she had an interesting life, she had spent most of it alone. There was no jealousy — simply a sincere interest.

Shared moments led to intimacy. Soon partings were accompanied by gentle hugs. When touched by a selection of music at a concert, Sue's hand would reach for Maryann's. Most meaningful of all were the glances between them when they shared a thought, a reaction to a movie, a moment of humor.

One movie that affected both women was "Terms of Endearment" (Paramount, 1983). Sue became very involved with the mother-daughter relationship between Aurora (Shirley MacLaine) and Emma (Debra Winger). Sue herself had experienced similar emotions with her own daughter as she was growing up. There were many disagreements but also shared interests and feelings. The intensity of this kind of relationship is unlike any other.

Maryann had no children and so this aspect of the story did not seem real to her. "How could a daughter be so irritated by her mother, yet have such closeness with her?" Maryann asked.

"It happens all the time," Sue said with a small chuckle. Sue was thinking of Maryann's volatile personality, her sense of fun, her warmth that could change to sudden bursts of anger for little or no apparent reason. Maryann always said it was when she was in pain that she was irritable. "It's not you, honey. It's me. When the pain comes back it makes me angry," Maryann would say.

Maryann could identify with Aurora's relationship with Garrett (Jack Nicholson), who was wild and crazy much of the time but who could be sensitive and caring when the situation called for it. Maryann had many brief romances with men — several of whom behaved in this way. She always felt that it was because she was a divorcee that men thought they could approach her in a sexy and somewhat crude manner. She was repulsed by this at first, but because of her sensuous nature, she soon became involved with them.

These very different kinds of experiences were evoked by the film, and Sue and Maryann enjoyed telling each other about them. They were glad when "Terms of Endearment" won many Academy Awards that April of 1984.

Maryann's physical condition went through good and bad periods. When she was in pain, she spent much of the time in her home, resting on a heating pad.

Sue visited her at times, and was moved by her friend's obvious discomfort. "Let me rub your neck, Maryann. I know it will make you feel better. It used to help Jack." Maryann resisted at first, but eventually she relaxed and enjoyed the massage.

We all need love, thought Sue. Affection can help to

relieve pain, just as it did for Jack. He would be glad to know that Maryann is here with me, making my loss easier to take.

Sue thought of Maryann many times when they were not together. If she read an interesting passage in a book, she thought, "I must show this to Maryann." A cloud formation or soft rain on a flower garden were things Sue wanted to share. Words to love songs kept coming into her head.

Sue thought, "Is it wrong to love a woman like that?" She felt that the way Maryann cared for Jack had something to do with it, but empathy and caring for another person — male or female — should be welcomed, no matter what evokes it.

After awhile, Maryann seemed to withdraw. She had other commitments. She was not readily available. The little drop-in visits were less frequent. Did Maryann feel that Sue had become too intimate? Or was the relationship between them solely dependent upon their shared feelings for Jack?

Finally Sue confronted her friend. "What has happened? You seem to be withdrawing from me lately. You had been so attentive since Jack died."

Maryann's answer was quick to come, and her voice was sharp. "I am not Jack, Sue. Don't make me a substitute lover."

Sue was startled. "What do you mean, Maryann? I don't expect you to take Jack's place — ever!"

"You know what I mean, Sue. It's all this hand-holding and hugging. I don't expect this from a woman."

"I do love you, Maryann. What's wrong with that? You have been so good to me and you're such a sweetie. Is it wrong to hug you? You always seem to welcome it."

"Maybe it doesn't seem wrong to you, Sue. It seems wrong to me. Actually, it frightens me."

"That's silly! I'm not going to hurt you or do anything

you don't want me to do. I don't expect you to be like Jack. I don't feel that way about you. Jack was strong. Someone I could lean on when things went wrong. You are very different. You are so vulnerable — so sensitive to things that are beautiful. I love to share these feelings with you. They are so easily detected. I think others respond to you like that. You seem to be asking for affection sometimes. And when you have aches and pains, I like to try to comfort you."

"I am not a tease, Sue. I don't purposely ask for affection. But you seem to want more than that. I am not used to women loving other women. After all, I come from a conventional, middle class family. People in our circle of friends were not gay or lesbian."

"Lesbian?" Sue was shocked. "Did I say anything about being a lesbian?" she shook her head slowly. "I have never thought of myself that way. I have had women friends with whom I have been close, but I never had an 'affair' nor a constant companion whom I could call a lover. As a matter of fact, I never went to bed with a woman."

Maryann shook her head. "That's not the point."

Sue continued, "Okay, I won't deny that some women interest me and I've always noticed those that are attractive and sensuous. You are one of those, Maryann, and I do love you in a way. But I don't want anything more from than the friendship we always had. Now that Jack is gone, it means much more to me because I need someone to share things with and someone who is concerned about me. Yes, I suppose, in a way you help fill the gap in my life that came about when Jack died. You are very important to me, but I don't want any more of a physical relationship that we already have. Does that make me a lesbian? I don't really know."

Maryann looked pensive and she now spoke in a soft

voice. "I do care about you, Sue, and I don't want to do or say anything that will hurt you. You know that."

The two women remained friends for about a year after this discussion. However, Sue was somewhat hesitant to show her affection. If she touched Maryann's hand lightly, she was quick to withdraw it after a second or two. Parting hugs were eliminated. But eye contact still had meaning, and many moments of enjoyment of theater, music and dining were still shared.

It was more than a year later when Sue came home from shopping to see her answering machine blinking at her. She recognized Maryann's voice. "I'm sorry I won't be able to go to the concert with you this weekend, honey. And I don't think I can go with you to Arizona either. Bye, now."

Sue was confused. Arizona? That was not where they planned to go together. No reason was given for these changes of plans. She called Maryann immediately, but the phone clicked off after her initial hello. Maryann's message had been so strange. Her voice sounded tense, but not angry. She stumbled over the word "Arizona" as if she had difficulty remember the name of the place they had planned to visit. The use of the affection term "honey" seemed inappropriate to the message.

This was actually the last communication between these friends. Sue was hurt and unbelieving. What had she done to bring this on? She tried several times to call Maryann, with the same result. On a few occasions when she saw Maryann at meetings, there was no eye contact and no conversation.

Sue tried to find out what happened by questioning some of their mutual friends. The reasons for the break were so minor that they seemed unreal. Sue had canceled a date at the last minute when she was not feeling well. Sue had not told Maryann about a class she had signed up for. Sue had not supported a resolution that Maryann had made at a meeting.

Sue remembered the time she had gone home after a movie when Maryann had expected her to come to her house to meet an out-of-town friend. Sue had a headache and was feeling depressed. "I'm sorry, sweetie." (She still used affectionate terms with Maryann.) "I really can't make it tonight. The movie reminded me of when I first met Jack. It really depressed me."

"But I expected you. I told Eva all about you and she's anxious to get to know you better."

"Some other time, Maryann. Give Eva my regards. Good night." Sue was vaguely aware that she didn't want to share Maryann with her old friend, Eva — not tonight, anyhow. Maryann's coolness to her over the past few weeks was bothering her. She would need to talk to Maryann alone before she was ready to spend a casual evening with her.

None of the reasons that Maryann gave made sense to Sue. Had her friend been annoyed that she didn't join them after the movie, that might be understandable. But it was not a reason to end a friendship completely. It was shortly after this that Sue received the phone call that broke off their relationship entirely.

It had been two years since Jack had died and the two friends had been so close during that time. Maryann was sensitive, and often offended by friends over small incidents. But this seemed ridiculous to Sue — so small a matter to cause so deep a hurt. She remembered the conversation about lesbianism they had. Can homophobia become so strong as to distort all reason? With no further explanations, this appeared to be so. Sue wondered who was the greater loser.

COMMENTS

Homophobia is defined by Webster (1988) as "irrational hatred or fear of homosexuals or homosexuality." It was not until 1972 that Weinberg coined the term and defined it as stated above. No lesbian or other non-heterosexually identified person fully escapes the effects of a society in which attitudes of homophobia seem to be deeply embedded.

A poll conducted by Newsweek Magazine in 1983 estimated that 66 percent of the U.S. population feel that homosexuality is an unacceptable lifestyle. A Gallup poll (1982) found that 59 percent of those surveyed would exclude homosexuals from teaching school, while 51 percent would not permit them to enter the clergy. (Blumenfeld & Raymond, 1988, p. 243) In a large national survey conducted by Roper Center, 73 percent of the respondents said that "sexual relations between two adults of the same sex are always wrong." (Davis & Smith, 1984) Therefore, to be a lesbian woman in our culture is to be a victim of stigma and discrimination.

So it is not surprising that Maryann reflects these societal attitudes. Having a basically liberal orientation, she would not admit to this prejudice. Very likely she found it necessary to find other reasons for her rejection of Sue. Her tension, possibly guilt, about these feelings is expressed in her telephone message and later in her total inability to confront Sue even in the most neutral of settings. Maryann is employing whatever defense mechanisms she can evoke to protect her own ego from the fear and anxiety resulting from her relationship with Sue.

In discussing the role of defensiveness in homophobia, Gregory M. Herek (Garnets & Kimmel, 1993, p. 318), says:

In psychodynamic terms, defensiveness involves an unconscious distortion of reality as a strategy for avoiding recognition of some unacceptable part of the self. One mode of defense is externalization of unacceptable characteristics through projection and other strategies.

Does Maryann herself experience some aspects of homosexual love for Sue? So much hostility in her rejection makes one think that she may be fighting aspects of her own personality which she finds difficult, or impossible, to acknowledge. This behavior is more commonly observed in males, whose macho image and athleticism may well be hiding homosexual tendencies. The character of the head master in the play, "Tea and Sympathy" is an example of a homosexual man whose defense was his own extreme masculinity.

Sue's unwillingness to admit to being a lesbian may be a naive unawareness on her part. Psychotherapists report on numerous incidents with clients where much denial is evident. One such dialogue reported by Slater (1995, p.140) follows:

My client has been talking about her friend Joanna for two sessions now. She appeared quite nervous and watched me intently, studying my face for reaction to her anecdotes of their friendship. Patiently, I waited for her to show me where she was leading us. Face flushed with anxiety, she said, "Joanna is actually a very special friend of mine," looking at me to see if I understood the code. "We aren't gay or anything, but we do express our love with physical affection." This was more code. "Are you letting me know that you two are sexually involved?" I asked. "I guess so," she said, "but not like actual lovers. We're both quite sure that we're not gay."

Women often turn to each other to fulfill voids that may exist in their marital life. Emotional intimacy is not frequently found even in successful marriages. "Best friends" among women are not ostracized by society as long as the women maintain the appearance of heterosexual relationships. Sue's recent widowhood and Maryann's empathy made them both ripe for this kind of "special friendship." For Maryann, the physical contact was too involving. Her own taboos may have made it seem unacceptable, even though she enjoyed it. For Sue, the relationship was a natural outgrowth of their closeness and emotional involvement.

Although both Sue and Maryann continue to believe they are not lesbians, Maryann sees Sue's affection in a different light, and considers it to be threatening to her own sense of self, possibly because of her natural responsiveness to it. A therapist might have helped to resolve these misunderstandings, but unfortunately, such an avenue for solution was not considered by either party.

REFERENCES

Blumenfeld, Warren J. and Diana Raymond. *Looking at Gay and Lesbian Life.* Boston: Beacon Press, 1988.

Davis, J.A. and Smith. *General Social surveys* (1972-1983) New Haven: Yale University, Roper Center for Public Opinion Research, 1984.

Garnets, Linda D. and Douglas C. Kimmel. *Psychological Perspectives on Lesbian and Gay Male Experiences.* New York: Columbia University Press, 1993.

Ruse, Michael. *Homosexuality: A Philosophical Inquiry.* New York: Blackwell, 1988.

Slater, Suzanne. *The Lesbian Family Life Cycle.* New York: The Free Press/ Simon and Schuster, 1995.

Webster's *New World Dictionary, Third College Edition.* Simon and Schuster, 1988.

Weinberg, George. *Society and the Healthy Homosexual.* New York: St. Martin's Press, 1972.

SEVEN

The 1990s

Senior Serenade

"I don't belong here," thought Charlotte as she was guided down the corridor by an attendant. The woman had a strong grip on her arm. "Does she think I'm going to try to get away?"

Shady Grove was one of the better nursing homes in the area. It was clean and there were lovely gardens with outdoor resting places. The food was good and nursing service was available twenty-four hours a day.

But the people! Everyone on walkers or in wheelchairs. All of the women wearing house dresses, slippers and cotton anklets. Most of them had gray hair, but some were blondes with gray or brown roots showing. Their hair was combed straight back or in braids. Whatever was easiest for the attendants to do. None wore makeup.

"What am I doing here?" Charlotte was well-groomed. She walked with a sure, lively step. She didn't need the attendant's help but the woman held on to her, saying she needed to show her where to go. Everyone they passed looked at her curiously. Some smiled feebly and said "Hello." One woman reached out and said, "Help me!" The attendant paid no attention.

Charlotte DID know why she was here. She had attempted suicide and failed. The doctors at the hospital where she had been taken refused to let her go home. Her son had arranged for her to go to Shady Grove, and it certainly was better than remaining in the psychiatric ward. Her two days there had been torture. No one treated her as a person, and she was herded from place to place like a helpless creature, like a dumb animal! Well, here at Shady Grove her family and friends could visit at selected hours, which is more than she could expect in the psychiatric ward.

Why did everyone, including her son, treat her as if she were out of her mind? Charlotte thought, "My reasoning in my notes to my friends was so logical. I don't believe in old age." Charlotte had been brought up as an only child in a household with three grandparents, one of whom was always ill. She knew the effects of this illness upon her mother, her father, and of course, on herself as a young child. Charlotte vowed, at the age of eight or nine, that she would never let this happen to her. She would not get old and sick and dependent. She would never have to rely on others to do everything for her.

At seventy, she was still in good shape — taking aerobics classes and swimming at an indoor pool twice a week, driving her own car and attending women's groups where she often led discussions. But how long can this go on? Many of Charlotte's friends were ill, two dying of cancer, three with Alzheimer's. Her husband had passed away last year, after many years with a debilitating disease. "Why wait for these things to happen to me?" she thought.

Her suicide action had been planned for a long time. She made the necessary financial arrangements and had saved sleeping pills. Charlotte had always had difficulty sleeping. and had been using sleeping pills for years. Unfortunately, she had not taken enough of them. She slept for a full day and woke up with a gash in her head. She didn't know how it happened, but there was blood all over her bed and in the bathroom. She called emergency. The paramedic who came saw some pills left on her night table and took them with him to the hospital. So they knew what she had done, and no one considered it rational.

Charlotte and the attendant reached the dining room where patients were being wheeled in and others were taking their places at long tables set with paper mats and dishes. There were plastic spoons, but no knives or forks. "We'll take you to your room and put your things away later," explained the attendance. "I'll come back for you," and she left.

Charlotte looked around. Most people began eating as soon as they were served, and there was little conversation. A man next to her nudged her arm and asked, "Did you just get here?" Without waiting for an answer, he stuffed a chicken leg into his mouth and chewed vigorously.

At the opposite end of the table, Charlotte noticed a woman looking at her and smiling. Her smile was not timid or weak. She nodded her head and raised one hand, fingers wiggling cheerily. "I don't know you, do I?" thought Charlotte. But there was something about her that was different. Her hair was gray, but it was short and curly. She sat in a wheelchair, but her back was straight and her head held high. Her eyes were bright as she gazed in Charlotte's direction.

The next time Charlotte saw this lady was later in the afternoon in the day room. She had unpacked her few belongings, rested a while and then was told she might go to the day room for some socializing. A small group sat around a TV watching a soap opera. Two men were playing checkers. Others were reading newspapers or magazines. There was little conversation.

The woman with the curly gray hair sat in her wheelchair by the window. A small table was in front of her and she was playing solitaire with a pack of old cards. She looked in Charlotte's direction as she came in. "Hi, do you want to play Gin?"

"I'd love to," Charlotte responded almost too eagerly.

"My name is Florence. Do you remember Judy Holiday in *Born Yesterday*, where she kept beating her friend at Gin?" Florence kept up a lively conversation as she shuffled the cards. Charlotte introduced herself and they began to play. Soon they were laughing aloud as one or the other called out, "Gin!" unexpectedly.

When juice and cookies were served a three o'clock, the women stopped their card game but continued to converse.

Florence told Charlotte that she had been in show business. "I was a Gypsy in a number of musicals and even had a couple of years with the Zigfield Follies."

"What is a Gypsy?" Charlotte asked. "Does that mean that you traveled around a lot?"

"Well, sort of," Florence answered. "'Gypsy' is a nickname for a chorus dancer in a show. I loved the theatre. There were a number of famous people that I remember from the old days. I was in the chorus of *Pajama Game* with Shirley MacLaine. She was pulled out to play the lead when Janis Paige got ill. We were all so excited for her. That was her big break, and she's been going strong ever since. Now she's playing character roles and it's hard to imagine what she was like in her Gypsy days. She used to send me Christmas cards, but not anymore. But tell me about you. You don't look like you belong here."

The lively pace of Florence's conversation was a little hard to follow, but now it seemed as if she had stopped and was waiting for Charlotte's reply.

Charlotte started out slowly. "My family thought I'd be better off here." But soon the truth came and she told Florence of her attempted suicide.

"Why did you do that?" Florence looked shocked.

"Well, I planned it when I was a child. I grew up with old people and decided that I never wanted to be old."

"Age doesn't matter," Florence responded. "It's how you feel inside — were you sad when you did it?"

"Not particularly. It was New Year's Eve and I had a few drinks with friends. I went home early to an empty apartment, but I didn't feel like going to bed. I watched a New Year's celebration on television and then got out some letters I had written to good friends. I decided to finish writing them. I wanted my son to mail them after I died."

"So that's when you decided to do that?" Florence asked.

"I really hadn't planned to do it right then. But I read over the letters, and suddenly I thought, 'Why not now? What reason do I have to go on and wait until I get really old?' So I took some pills I had been saving. I was really surprised when I woke up a whole day later and found my pillow full of blood. I still don't know how it happened. I discovered a gash in my head, and I called 911. I ended up in the hospital and after I was stitched up I was taken to the psychiatric ward. I guess the pill containers on my night table gave me away. I was lucky that my son was notified and he was able to arrange to bring me here."

"It's nice that you have a son who cares for you," Florence responded. "I don't have any children. I was married for a while, but my husband left me to live with his boyfriend. I knew he was gay, but he was such a sweet guy and we had some good times together. We were friends until he died a few years ago. Do you have a husband?"

"No, I'm a widow. It's been over a year now. My husband

had Parkinson's Disease and the last few years of his life were difficult for both of us. I'm living alone now, and quite frankly, I don't like it."

Florence looked concerned. "I know what it is to be lonely. Anyhow, I'm glad you are here for my sake!"

The women met daily and even arranged to sit next to each other at meal times. Charlotte looked forward to these meetings. Florence was the only lively person in the entire place, and she was always so cheerful. It made Charlotte feel guilty for her own attitude which led to her suicide attempt. Florence had no family, and had multiple sclerosis from the time she was forty. She had odd jobs after her dancing career ended — addressing envelopes at home or as a part-time office worker or receptionist — anything to bring in a small income. People who spend the most productive years of their lives in the theatre usually have no insurance and little security. A friend had arranged to get her on Medicaid and so, after a long wait, she was able to get into Shady Grove. Since she reached sixty-five, she had been able to get a small allowance from Social Security, most of which money went to the nursing home. She was so grateful to be here and was so glad for anything to do or anyone to talk to.

There were some planned activities at Shady Grove. An arts and crafts class met two mornings a week, and exercises that could be done sitting down were given three alternate days. On Monday afternoons there were movies, usually old classics that both of the women enjoyed. In the sad parts, Charlotte often reached over to hold Florence's hand. The fingers were bony, but there was a pulse Charlotte could feel — a soft, steady beat. Florence's hand moved slightly in response to Charlotte's touch and frequently their fingers intertwined affectionately.

When Charlotte's son came on Sunday, he brought a small

television set for her room. Charlotte asked if Florence could move in and become her roommate. The staff welcomed this suggestion since they preferred to have two patients in a room. Charlotte's first roommate had left at the end of her first week there and a replacement had not been made as yet. Also, Charlotte could push Florence's wheelchair to the dining room which relieved the attendants to care for others.

Now the friends could spend all of their time together. They soon knew a great deal about each other. They found that they both had always been interested in women.

"I remember, when I was a kid, I always had a special girlfriend in whom I could confide," Charlotte said. "Sometimes it was an older girl, like a counselor at camp, whom I worshipped from afar."

"I went to the movies a lot when I was a kid," Florence contributed her reminiscences. "I always paid more attention to the actresses than I did to the actors."

"I was like that, too," Charlotte confessed.

Neither of the women ever considered herself a lesbian. They liked men and lived with men. But the attraction to other women had always been there. It was the first time Charlotte had admitted this to anyone. In her respectable middle class life, no one ever talked about these kinds of things. In many ways, Florence was more worldly, although she had little formal education.

"When I was married, many of our friends were gay. I found out about my husband in our first year together, and we remained married for ten years after that. We both were in show business so we had a good deal in common. Our friends were both gay and straight and there were several lesbian couples we knew. Of course, there is more of that today, and it is more acceptable. I suppose if I were younger today I would have a different lifestyle than I had."

Charlotte responded casually, "I had read in current women's magazines that homosexuality was more common that is usually supposed. Somewhere I remember reading that over sixty percent of people interviewed admitted to homosexual thoughts and fantasies. A scientist reported that most mammalian animals are bisexual at times, so why not us?"

Florence nodded in agreement. "So you're not shocked or surprised at my confessions?"

"No, not at all," Charlotte said.

After these open discussions between them, the two women permitted themselves more physical contact. They were careful not to be noticed in the day room because attendants were sure to talk among themselves. But at night, when they could close their door, they frequently got into bed together to watch old movies on television. A favorite of theirs was "Turning Point" (20th Century Fox, 1977).

"I know how Emma must have felt when she realized that she had sacrificed having a family to continue her career in dance." Florence could easily identify with this role, played by Anne Bancroft.

Charlotte gave Florence a small hug and then let her fingers run through Charlotte's short curly hair. When she was tired, this frequently put Florence to sleep. Little purring noises, like a small pussy-cat, let Charlotte know that her friend was enjoying this. With legs intertwined and Florence's head on her shoulder, Charlotte was able to get to sleep more readily than she ever had been able to do before.

"I never thought I could be happy here," Charlotte thought. "How fortunate we are to have found each other."

COMMENTS

Sexual orientation may change at various stages of life. "One can have the same-sex attraction or sexual experience in childhood, adolescence, the 20s and 30s, and not label oneself 'lesbian' until midlife or older. Then there are those women who knew they were lesbians when they were younger but who did not act on it until midlife or old age. Some have no history of attraction to women until midlife or older." (Sang, 1991, as quoted in Dworkin, Sara ad Fernando J. Guitierrez, 1992)

According to her account, Charlotte was always attracted to women but lived a heterosexual lifestyle throughout a long marriage. Some of her friendships may have been "romantic", but there was no admission to lesbianism, and perhaps Charlotte and her friend were not even aware of the physical aspects of their relationships. Obviously sex is not the sole basis for these attachments.

Florence, on the other hand, may have had previous sexual attachments to women. She traveled in mixed homosexual and heterosexual circles. Her husband was gay, and no doubt, had encounters with his male friend while still married to Florence. What opportunities were available to Florence and if she pursued them is not known. Certainly with the onset of her deteriorating disease, her opportunities became less feasible. She welcomed Charlotte as a companion and lover, and seemed to have no qualms about it.

There have been several recent studies of aging lesbians, e.g. Monica Keho's "Lesbians Over 60 Speak for Themselves." Some had long-term relationships. Others found suitable companions in later life. Many accepted themselves as lesbians, but had not found suitable lovers. One case study, reported in the literature (ibid. p. 44) was a 68-year-old woman, Roz, who acknowledge her lesbianism all of her life. After a cancer operation, she came to the conclusion that the only way she was going to continue living was if she had a significant other. Roz was determined to find that special someone.

Because most of her close friends had died and she was no longer on speaking terms with others, she was socially isolated. She joined a peer group sponsored by a gay and lesbian senior organization. After meeting a woman her age, they planned a future together. But things went down hill when Roz became critical of everything her partner did. She did not like her companion's friends who were never intellectual enough; she did not like the way she dressed, etc. Just because one is an older lesbian does not mean that one will have something in common with other older lesbians. Unfortunately, many older women are bitter about their lives, and critical of others.

Certainly, finding a suitable mate at a late stage of life is a blessing. Since women outnumber men in the years above 65, a lesbian relationship should be welcomed. While it was once considered that homosexuals were doomed to a life of unhappiness, recent research has established that most older lesbians enjoy life, are more physically active and are more accepting of age than their heterosexual counterparts.

REFERENCES

Dworkin, Sara H. and Fernando J. Gutierrez. *Counseling Gay Men and Lesbians.* Alexandria, VA: American Association for Counseling and Development, 1992.

Hanna, Judith Lynne. *Dance, Sex and Gender: Signs of Identity, Dominance, Defiance and Desire.* Chicago, IL: University of Chicago Press, 1988.

Keho, Monica. *Lesbians Over 60 Speak For Themselves.* New York: The Haworth Press, 1989.

Lee, John Alan. *Gay Midlife and Maturity.* New York: The Haworth Press, 1989.

Maddox, Brenda. *Married and Gay.* New York: Harcourt, Brace Jovanowich, 1982.

Slater, Suzanne. *The Lesbian Family Life Cycle.* New York: Simon and Schuster/ The Free Press, 1995.

Unruh, David. Invisible Lives: Social Worlds of the Aged. *Beverly Hills, CA: Sage Publishing Co., 1983.*